Grade 1

Addison-Wesley Mathematics

Challenges Workbook

▲▲ **Addison-Wesley Publishing Company**

*Menlo Park, California ■ Reading, Massachusetts ■ New York
Don Mills, Ontario ■ Wokingham, England ■ Amsterdam ■ Bonn
Sydney ■ Singapore ▶ Tokyo ■ Madrid ■ San Juan*

ISBN 0-201-27111-7

3 4 5 6 7 8 9 10 - HC - 95 94 93 92 91

Table of Contents

Name _____

Where Is It?

1. Is the toy on the **top** or on the **bottom**?
Draw a line to show where each toy is.

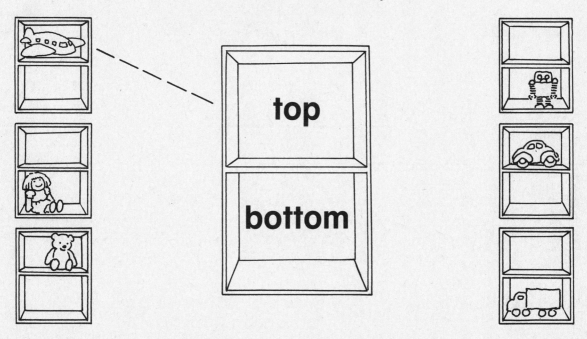

2. Is the ball **in** or **out**?
Draw a line to show where each ball is.

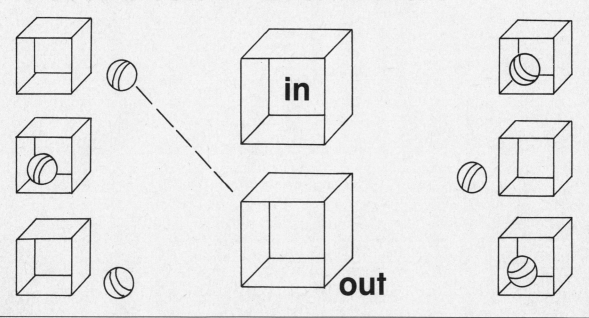

Pattern Blocks

Work with a partner.
Use pattern blocks.

One partner makes a pattern with blocks.

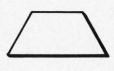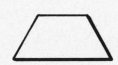

The other partner draws the pattern.

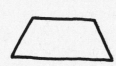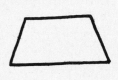

Make 2 patterns.

Each partner takes a turn making and drawing a pattern.

1.

_____

2.

_____

Choose one of your patterns.
Can you show it by clapping and snapping?

Name _____

Fun With Patterns

Count the dots in each space. Then color.

Color 1 [blue ▷]   2 [yellow ▷]   3 [pink ▷]   4 [green ▷]

Name _____

Number Cube Toss

Use the girl's numbers.
Write and continue a pattern.

1. __3__ , __5__ , __3__ , _____ , _____ , _____

Toss 2 number cubes.
Write your numbers.
Continue the pattern.

2. _____ , _____ , _____ , _____ , _____ , _____

3. _____ , _____ , _____ , _____ , _____ , _____

Now toss 3 number cubes. Write your numbers.
Continue the pattern.

4. _____ , _____ , _____ , _____ , _____ , _____

5. _____ , _____ , _____ , _____ , _____ , _____

Use with text pages 7 – 8.

Name _____

How Are These Different?

Work with a partner.
Talk about the patterns.
Ring the one-difference pattern in each exercise.

1.

2.

3. Use blocks to make a one-difference pattern.
Draw and color your pattern.
Show it to your partner.

Name _____

Number Card Patterns

You need two sets of number
cards 5 to 9 and a partner.
Work together to arrange
these cards in a pattern.
Record the pattern.

| 5 | 5 | 6 | 6 |

_____ , _____ , _____ , _____

Can you find another pattern?
Record it.

_____ , _____ , _____ , _____

Use these cards.

| 7 | 7 | 8 | 8 | 9 | 9 |

See how many patterns you can find.
Record your patterns.

_____ , _____ , _____ , _____ , _____ , _____

_____ , _____ , _____ , _____ , _____ , _____

_____ , _____ , _____ , _____ , _____ , _____

_____ , _____ , _____ , _____ , _____ , _____

_____ , _____ , _____ , _____ , _____ , _____

_____ , _____ , _____ , _____ , _____ , _____

Name _____

Count the Coins

Dear Family,
    We have been studying numbers to 9, patterns, and pennies and nickels. Help your child use coins to complete these exercises. Observe to see if your child recognizes the value of a penny and nickel.

Work with a family member.

Use 1 and 9 .

Write how much money.

1.

3   ___ ___
                           − − − ¢

2.

1 2   ___ ___
                                                    − − − ¢

3.

1 3   ___ ___
                                                  − − − ¢

4.

8   ___ ___
                           − − − ¢

5.

6   ___ ___
                           − − − ¢

6.

1  4   ___ ___
                             − − − ¢

Name _____

Counting on the Calculator

Look at your . Fill in each key.

1. Press. Write what you see.

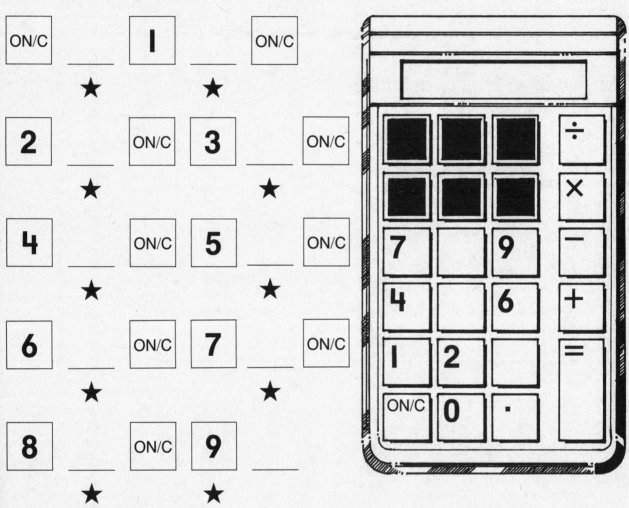

ON/C	___	I	___	ON/C
	★		★	
2	___	ON/C	3	___	ON/C
	★		★	
4	___	ON/C	5	___	ON/C
	★		★	
6	___	ON/C	7	___	ON/C
	★		★	
8	___	ON/C	9	___	
	★		★	

2. Start at the top.
Write each number above a ★ in a ☐.

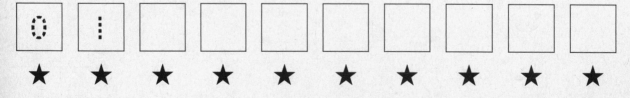

Counting Before and After

1. What number comes

after 7? [8]   after 2? [ ]

after 8? [ ]   after 6? [ ]

after 5? [ ]   after 4? [ ]

---

2. What number comes

before 5? [4]   before 8? [ ]

before 9? [ ]   before 3? [ ]

before 6? [ ]   before 7? [ ]

Name _____

Tally Up!

Play with a partner. Take turns.
Decide how many to draw. Draw the objects.
Tally to find how many.
Write the number for each group.

1. Draw balls.

Tally   Number

2. Draw stars.

3. Draw fish.

Making Groups

1. Write how many.

2 groups of 5 and 2 extras	2 groups of 5	2 groups of 5 and 1 extra

2. Take 12 counters.
Show the groups and extras.
Draw a picture and write how many.

2 groups of 5 and 2 extra	2 groups of 5

2 groups of 5 and 1 extra	1 group of 10 and 2 extra

Designing Numbers

1. Write how many in each design.

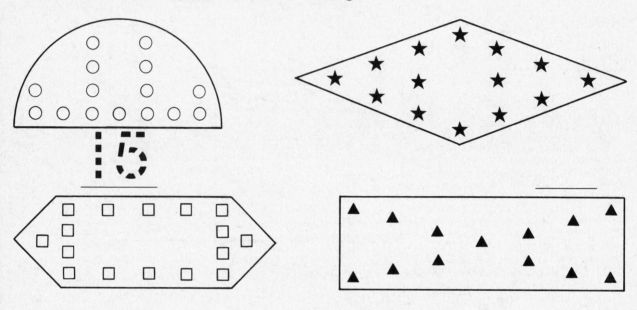

2. Draw your own designs to match the numbers.

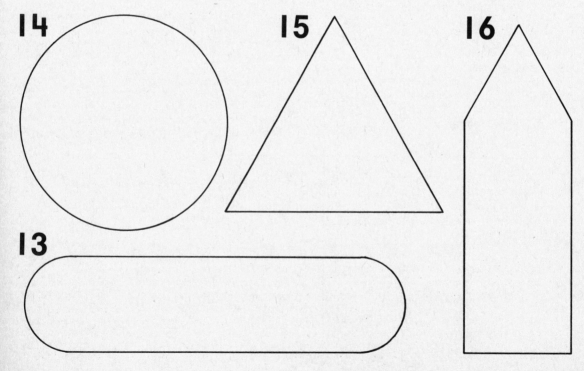

14   15   16

13

Name _____

Counting Maze

How many of each?
Cross out as you count.
Write the numbers.

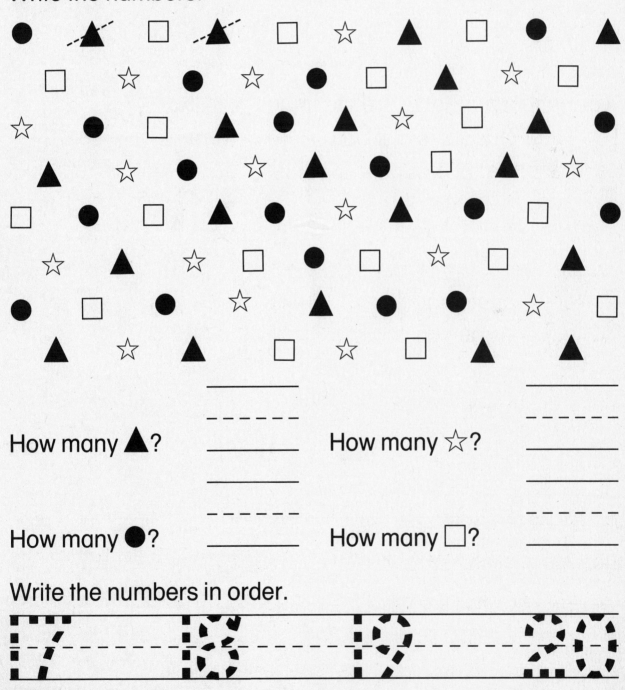

How many ▲? _____   How many ☆? _____

How many ●? _____   How many □? _____

Write the numbers in order.

17   18   19   20

Name _____

Shopping

Work with a partner. One student is the store clerk.
The other student is a shopper. Take turns.
Each shopper has punchout coins.

Go shopping.
Use coins to pay the clerk.
Buy as much as you can.

_____

Draw to show what you bought.

_____

Draw to show what coins you have left.

_____
_____

Name _____

More or Less?

Work with a partner. Use counters.
Take turns telling stories about the pictures.
Put a ✔ to tell what happens. Write the answer.

1.

What happens?

☐ You find one. ☐ You lose one.

(I more I less)

How many now?
_____
- - - - - - - - - - - - - -
_____

2.

What happens?

☐ One comes. ☐ One leaves.

(I more I less)

How many now?
_____
- - - - - - - - - - - - - -
_____

3.

What happens?

☐ You pick one. ☐ You eat one.

(I more I less)

How many now?
_____
- - - - - - - - - - - - - -
_____

Favorite Fruit

Dear Family,
  Our class has been learning to read and make bar graphs. Observe as your child completes this graph. Check to see if he or she is shading one space on the graph for each response. Then help by writing your child's answers to the questions.

Ask your family members to choose their favorite fruit. Show their answers on the graph.

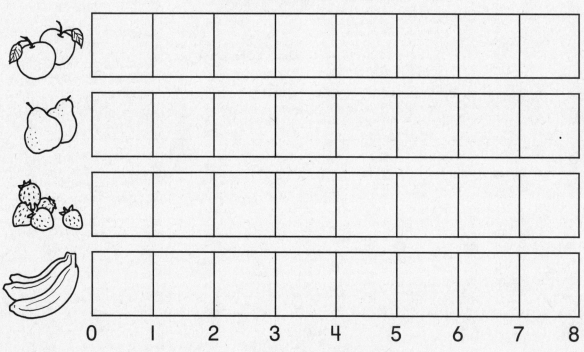

Which Is Your Favorite Fruit?

Ask a family member to write your answers.

1. Which fruit did most family members choose?

_____

2. How did you take your survey?

_____

So Many Fish

Color a ☐ for each tally.

 HHH I    HHH III

 II    IIII

Number of Different Fish

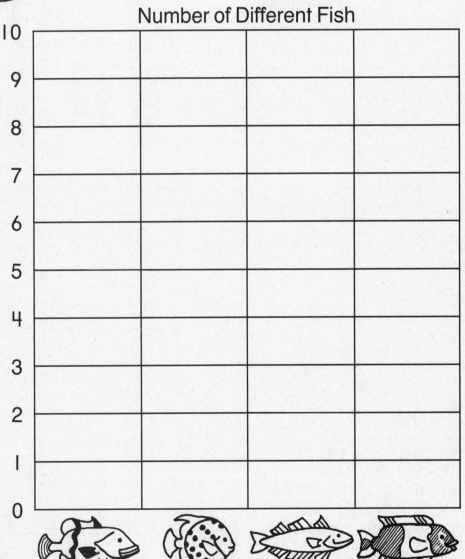

How many fish are there in all? _____ fish

Name _____

Counting Backward

Use your 🖩 .

1. Start at 10.
Count backward to 5.
Press.

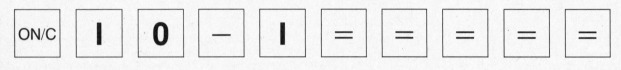

Write. _9_ _8_ ___ ___ ___

2. Start at 15.
Count backward to 10.
Press.

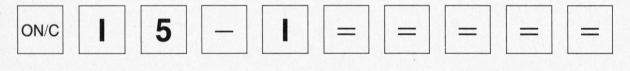

Write. ___ ___ ___ ___ ___

3. Start at 20.
Count backward to 15.
Press.

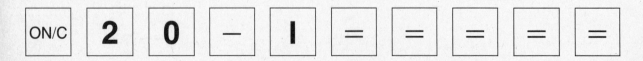

Write. ___ ___ ___ ___ ___

Story Time

Play with a partner.
Tell a story about the picture.
Your partner writes the number you say.
Then your partner retells the story
with a number that is more.

Write the number. Take turns going first.

1.

_ _ _ _   _ _ _ _

2.

_ _ _ _   _ _ _ _

3.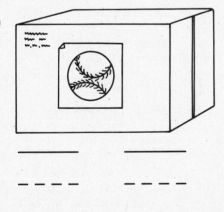

_ _ _ _   _ _ _ _

4.

_ _ _ _   _ _ _ _

Number Stories

Make cards like these.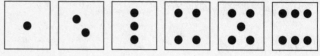
Place all cards in a row facedown.
Turn over 2 cards.
Draw what you see. Write a number story.

1.

☐ and ☐

___ + ___ ___
in all

2.

☐ and ☐

___ + ___ ___
in all

3.

☐ and ☐

___ + ___ ___
in all

4.

☐ and ☐

___ + ___ ___
in all

5.

☐ and ☐

___ + ___ ___
in all

6.

☐ and ☐

___ + ___ ___
in all

Drawing More

Draw some more in the box.
Write the addition sentence to match.

1.

 + 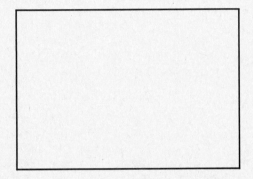 $3 + \underline{\quad} = \underline{\quad}$
sum

2.

 + 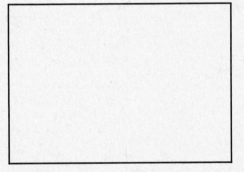 $1 + \underline{\quad} = \underline{\quad}$
sum

3.

 + 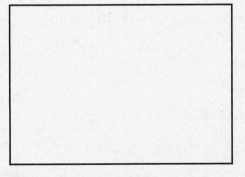 $2 + \underline{\quad} = \underline{\quad}$
sum

Name _____

Sum Race

Play with a partner.

Use your spinner.

Put a marker at START.

Take turns.

Spin. Tell the sum.

Move that number of spaces.

Keep playing until you reach FINISH.

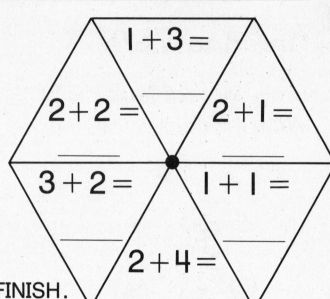

$1+3=$

$2+2=$

$2+1=$

$3+2=$

$1+1=$

$2+4=$

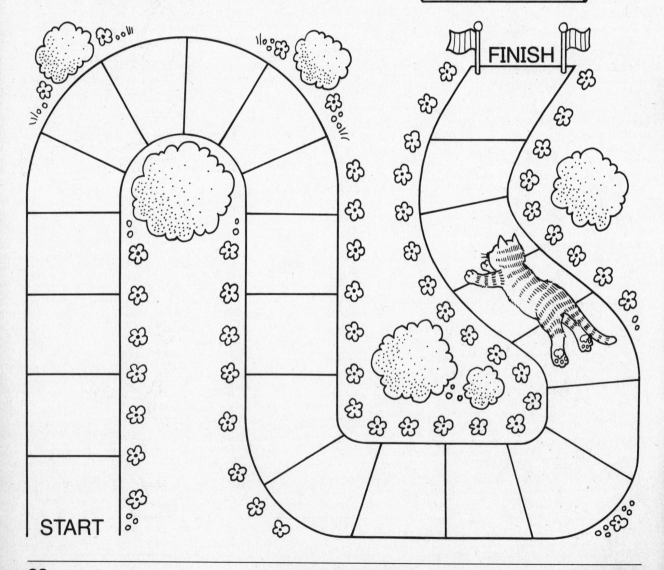

FINISH

START

Name _____

Some Sums

Draw ● to make the sum.
Write the missing numbers.

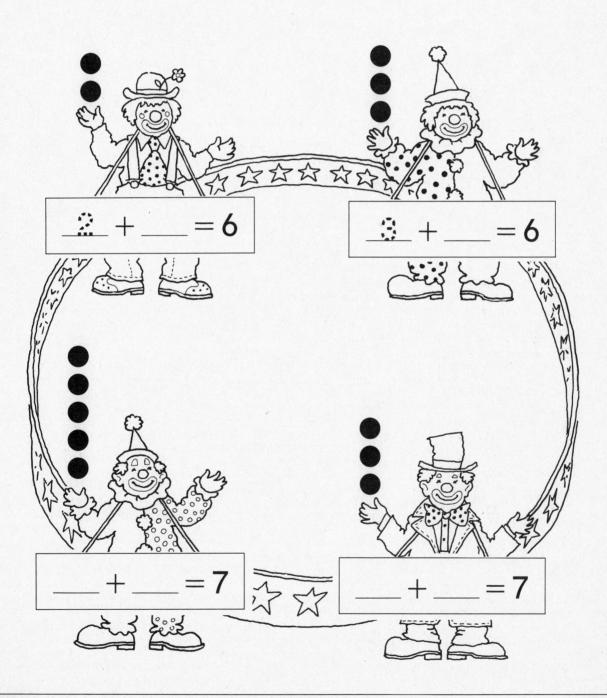

$\underline{2} + \underline{} = 6$

$\underline{3} + \underline{} = 6$

$\underline{} + \underline{} = 7$

$\underline{} + \underline{} = 7$

Name _____

Party Time

Read each story.
Write a number sentence.
Answer the question.

1. Jim has 2 balloons.
Nan has 3 balloons. ____ ◯ ____ □ ____

How many do they have in all? ____ balloons

2. There were 4 girls at the party.
There were 2 boys at the party. ____ ◯ ____ □ ____

How many were at the party in all? ____ children

3. The cake has 6 little candles.
It has 1 big candle. ____ ◯ ____ □ ____

How many candles are on the cake? ____ candles

Name _____

Turnaround Facts

Complete the number sentence.
Then write it another way using turnaround facts.
Color all the names for 3 blue.
Color all the names for 4 red.
Color all the names for 5 green.

$3 + 1 = 4$

$\underline{1} + \underline{3} = \underline{4}$

$2 + 3 = \underline{}$

$\underline{} + \underline{} = \underline{}$

$1 + 2 = \underline{}$

$\underline{} + \underline{} = \underline{}$

$1 + 4 = \underline{}$

$\underline{} + \underline{} = \underline{}$

$0 + 4 = \underline{}$

$\underline{} + \underline{} = \underline{}$

$1 + 3 = \underline{}$

$\underline{} + \underline{} = \underline{}$

$2 + 2 = \underline{}$

$\underline{} + \underline{} = \underline{}$

$5 + 0 = \underline{}$

$\underline{} + \underline{} = \underline{}$

$0 + 3 = \underline{}$

$\underline{} + \underline{} = \underline{}$

$3 + 2 = \underline{}$

$\underline{} + \underline{} = \underline{}$

Creating Addition Facts

Write your own exercises
for each sum.
Make each one different.

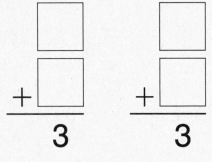

1.

$$\begin{array}{r} \square \\ +\ \square \\ \hline 3 \end{array} \qquad \begin{array}{r} \square \\ +\ \square \\ \hline 3 \end{array} \qquad \begin{array}{r} \square \\ +\ \square \\ \hline 3 \end{array}$$

2.

$$\begin{array}{r} \square \\ +\ \square \\ \hline 4 \end{array} \qquad \begin{array}{r} \square \\ +\ \square \\ \hline 4 \end{array} \qquad \begin{array}{r} \square \\ +\ \square \\ \hline 4 \end{array} \qquad \begin{array}{r} \square \\ +\ \square \\ \hline 4 \end{array} \qquad \begin{array}{r} \square \\ +\ \square \\ \hline 4 \end{array}$$

3.

$$\begin{array}{r} \square \\ +\ \square \\ \hline 5 \end{array} \qquad \begin{array}{r} \square \\ +\ \square \\ \hline 5 \end{array} \qquad \begin{array}{r} \square \\ +\ \square \\ \hline 5 \end{array} \qquad \begin{array}{r} \square \\ +\ \square \\ \hline 5 \end{array} \qquad \begin{array}{r} \square \\ +\ \square \\ \hline 5 \end{array}$$

Name _____

Playing Store

Work in a group of 3.
One student is the store clerk.
Two students are shoppers.
See how much fruit each can buy.
You each have 10 pennies to spend.

Draw a picture to show what you buy.
Write how much you spend.

Ask the store clerk to check your work.
Now give the clerk a turn at shopping.
Tell who spent more money in your group.

Books and More Books

Match the story with the correct picture.
Then write the problem and solve.

1. Kim had 4 books.
She got 1 more book.
How many does
she have now?

＋ ____

_____ books ____

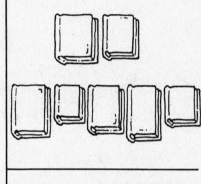

2. Paco read 3 books.
Then he read 2 more.
How many books did
Paco read in all?

＋ ____

_____ books ____

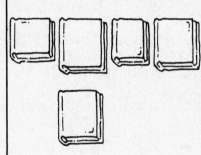

3. Maria put 2 books on the
rack. She put 5 books on
the shelf. How many books
did Maria put away?

＋ ____

_____ books ____

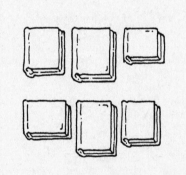

4. Ted had 3 books.
Al had 3 books.
How many books
did the boys have?

＋ ____

_____ books ____

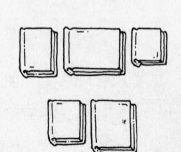

Name _____

Shapes, Shapes, Shapes

Write how many in all.
Cover some.
Write a number story.

shapes in all	take away	number story	
1. ___5___	all ☐	___ − ___	___ are left
2. ___	all ◯	___ − ___	___ are left
3. ___	all ■ and ◯	___ − ___	___ are left

shapes in all	take away	number story	
4. ___	all ☐	___ − ___	___ are left
5. ___	all ◯	___ − ___	___ are left
6. ___	all △ and ◯	___ − ___	___ are left

Name _____

There They Go!

Count how many in all.
Color the ones that go away.
Finish the number sentence.

1.

4 − 1 = 3

2.

___ − ___ = ___

3.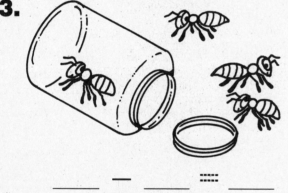

___ − ___ = ___

4.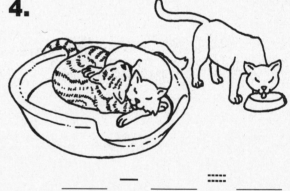

___ − ___ = ___

5.

___ − ___ = ___

6.

___ − ___ = ___

Name _____

Coloring the Clouds

Subtract. Then color.

1 yellow
2 orange
3 brown
4 green

$$\begin{array}{r} 3 \\ -1 \\ \hline \end{array}$$

$$\begin{array}{r} 6 \\ -2 \\ \hline \end{array}$$

$$\begin{array}{r} 5 \\ -4 \\ \hline \end{array}$$

$$\begin{array}{r} 4 \\ -3 \\ \hline \end{array}$$

$$\begin{array}{r} 5 \\ -3 \\ \hline \end{array}$$

$$\begin{array}{r} 4 \\ -2 \\ \hline \end{array}$$

$$\begin{array}{r} 4 \\ -1 \\ \hline \end{array}$$

$$\begin{array}{r} 5 \\ -2 \\ \hline \end{array}$$

$$\begin{array}{r} 6 \\ -3 \\ \hline \end{array}$$

$$\begin{array}{r} 2 \\ -1 \\ \hline \end{array}$$

$$\begin{array}{r} 5 \\ -1 \\ \hline \end{array}$$

$$\begin{array}{r} 3 \\ -2 \\ \hline \end{array}$$

Name _____

Away They Go

Dear Family,
 Our class has been learning how to subtract. Read these stories to your child. Help him or her draw objects, cross some out to subtract, and count the number remaining. Then write how many are left.

1. 3 boats are on the lake. I boat sailed away. How many boats are still there?

$$\begin{array}{r} 3 \\ -\,1 \\ \hline \end{array}$$

2. The children are flying 5 kites. 2 kites got away. How many kites do the children still have?

$$\begin{array}{r} 5 \\ -\,2 \\ \hline \end{array}$$

3. The children are playing with 4 balls. 3 balls rolled into the lake. How many balls do the the children still have?

$$\begin{array}{r} 4 \\ -\,3 \\ \hline \end{array}$$

4. The children caught 6 fish. 3 fish jumped back into the lake. How many fish do the children have now?

$$\begin{array}{r} 6 \\ -\,3 \\ \hline \end{array}$$

Write Your Own

Write your own exercises.
Make each one different.
Subtract. Look for a pattern.

1.

$$\begin{array}{r} 3 \\ -\ 0 \\ \hline 3 \end{array} \qquad \begin{array}{r} 3 \\ -\ 1 \\ \hline 2 \end{array} \qquad \begin{array}{r} 3 \\ -\ 2 \\ \hline 1 \end{array} \qquad \begin{array}{r} 3 \\ -\ 3 \\ \hline 0 \end{array}$$

2.

$$\begin{array}{r} 4 \\ -\ \square \\ \hline \end{array} \qquad \begin{array}{r} 4 \\ -\ \square \\ \hline \end{array} \qquad \begin{array}{r} 4 \\ -\ \square \\ \hline \end{array} \qquad \begin{array}{r} 4 \\ -\ \square \\ \hline \end{array} \qquad \begin{array}{r} 4 \\ -\ \square \\ \hline \end{array}$$

3.

$$\begin{array}{r} 5 \\ -\ \square \\ \hline \end{array} \qquad \begin{array}{r} 5 \\ -\ \square \\ \hline \end{array} \qquad \begin{array}{r} 5 \\ -\ \square \\ \hline \end{array} \qquad \begin{array}{r} 5 \\ -\ \square \\ \hline \end{array} \qquad \begin{array}{r} 5 \\ -\ \square \\ \hline \end{array} \qquad \begin{array}{r} 5 \\ -\ \square \\ \hline \end{array}$$

Name _____

Using a Code

| 7 | 6 | 5 | 4 | 3 | 2 | I | 0 |

Use the code to fill in the numbers.
Subtract. Match related facts.

7 − 5 = 2

☐ − ☐ = ___

☐ − ☐ = ___

☐ − ☐ = ___

☐ − ☐ = ___

7 − 2 = 5

☐ − ☐ = ___

☐ − ☐ = ___

☐ − ☐ = ___

☐ − ☐ = ___

Name _____

Fun with Families

Dear Family,
   In our math book we have completed a lesson on fact families. As your child completes this page, encourage discussion about what he or she is doing. Then gather several related objects (such as stuffed animals or toy cars) about which your child can write a fact family.

Write a fact family for  .

___ + ___ = ___   ___ − ___ = ___

___ + ___ = ___   ___ − ___ = ___

Draw a picture story for 1 of the facts.

Tell your story to a family member.
Have the family member write your story.

Get 3, 4, 5, or 6 things at home.
Make a fact family about these things.
Write your number sentences here.

___ + ___ = ___   ___ − ___ = ___

___ + ___ = ___   ___ − ___ = ___

Add or Subtract

Think about whether to add or subtract.
Draw more pictures or cross out some.
Write a fact to solve.

1. Rick picked 3 oranges.

   He picked 2 more.

   How many does he have in all? _____ oranges

   $$\begin{array}{r} \underline{} \\ + \\ \hline \end{array}$$

2. Su Li had 6 flowers.

   She gave away 2.

   How many does she have left? _____ flowers

   $$\begin{array}{r} \underline{} \\ - \\ \hline \end{array}$$

3. Ken had 4 stamps.

   He used all of them.

   How many does he have left? _____ stamps

   $$\begin{array}{r} \underline{} \\ - \\ \hline \end{array}$$

4. Melissa found 5 shells.

   Then she found another one.

   How many does she have now? _____ shells

   $$\begin{array}{r} \underline{} \\ + \\ \hline \end{array}$$

Name _____

Who Am I?
Read each clue.
Write the secret number.

1. I am 2 more than 5.

_____

2. I am 1 more than 4.

_____

3. I am 2 more than 8.

_____

4. I am 2 more than 7.

_____

5. I am 1 more than 9.

_____

6. I am 3 more than 8.

_____

7. I am 2 more than 10.

_____

8. I am 1 more than 0.

_____

9. I am 3 more than 11.

_____

10. I am 2 more than 6.

_____

Name _____

Touchdown, Turnaround

Dear Family,
   Our class has been learning about turnaround facts. Turnaround facts are two ways to write the same sum, such as $8 + 2$ and $2 + 8$. Write the numbers 0 to 8 on a piece of paper and cut them out. Put the numbers 0 to 2 in one pile and 3 to 8 in another. Observe as your child uses the numbers to make up turnaround facts. Record the stories your child makes up. Then read them aloud and talk about them together.

Work with a family member. Pick a number from each pile.

Write an addition fact.   ____ + ____ = ____
Tell a story about your number sentence.
Have a family member write it.

Write the turnaround fact here.   ____ + ____ = ____
Tell a story about this number sentence.
Have a family member write it.

Read the stories aloud.
Talk about them. Tell how they are alike.

Name _____

What a Card!

Play with a partner.
Make number cards for 1 to 10.
Put them facedown.
Take turns. Choose a number card.
Each card is the answer to one of the
number sentences below.
Find the sentence and place
your card on the board.
The game ends when the board is covered.

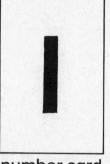

number card

5 + 3 = ___	3 + 2 = ___
1 + 0 = ___	2 + 1 = ___
4 + 2 = ___	3 + 7 = ___
1 + 3 = ___	0 + 2 = ___
3 + 6 = ___	2 + 5 = ___

Make a Match

Use numbers from the basket to complete each addition sentence.

1.

___ + ___ = 8

___ + ___ = 4

___ + ___ = 5

___ + ___ = 9

2.

___ + ___ = 7

___ + ___ = 11

___ + ___ = 6

___ + ___ = 10

3.

___ + ___ = 7

___ + ___ = 12

___ + ___ = 8

___ + ___ = 9

4.

___ + ___ = 9

___ + ___ = 8

___ + ___ = 10

___ + ___ = 11

Name _____

Spin a Sum

Play with a partner.
Take turns spinning.
Each partner writes the spin
number in a ☐.
Add. Ring the greater sum.

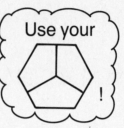
Use your !

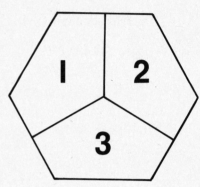

Put a check if the sums are the same.

1. $4 + \boxed{} = \underline{}$

   $4 + \boxed{} = \underline{} \ \boxed{}$

2. $5 + \boxed{} = \underline{}$

   $5 + \boxed{} = \underline{} \ \boxed{}$

3. $3 + \boxed{} = \underline{}$

   $3 + \boxed{} = \underline{} \ \boxed{}$

4. $8 + \boxed{} = \underline{}$

   $8 + \boxed{} = \underline{} \ \boxed{}$

5. $9 + \boxed{} = \underline{}$

   $9 + \boxed{} = \underline{} \ \boxed{}$

6. $7 + \boxed{} = \underline{}$

   $7 + \boxed{} = \underline{} \ \boxed{}$

Bear's House

Play with a partner.
Each puts a counter on Baby Bear.
Take turns spinning a number.
Move your counter that many spaces.
Then add the number on the spinner
to the number you land on.
Say the sum. Your partner checks.
Play until you both reach the bears' house.

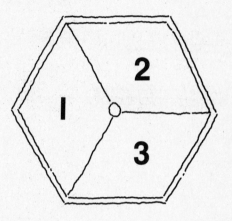

Name _____

It's a Toss Up [7]

Toss two number cubes.
Add the numbers on top.
Write the fact.

Cube 1 [7] [8] [9] [7] [8] [9]
Cube 2 [1] [2] [3] [1] [2] [3]

1. ___ + ___ = ___   2. ___ + ___ = ___

3. ___ + ___ = ___   4. ___ + ___ = ___

5. ___ + ___ = ___   6. ___ + ___ = ___

7. ___ + ___ = ___   8. ___ + ___ = ___

9. ___ + ___ = ___   10. ___ + ___ = ___

Look at the sums above. Tally to show the sums.

sums of 8 _____   sums of 9 _____

sums of 10 _____   sums of 11 _____

sums of 12 _____

Color the graph to show the data.

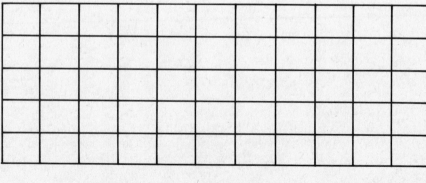

sums of 8
sums of 9
sums of 10
sums of 11
sums of 12

0 1 2 3 4 5 6 7 8 9 10

Name _____

Tell a Story

Work with a partner.
Take turns telling a story about the picture.
Write the addition or subtraction sentence that
matches your partner's story.

1. the story

2. the 🙂🙂 story

_____

_____

3. the ⛵ story

4. the story

_____

_____

Twice as Many

Read the question. Write how many.

1. How many wheels are there on 2 cars?

_____

2. How many wheels are there on 2 bicycles?

_____

3. How many legs are there on 2 dogs?

_____

4. How many fingers are there on 2 hands?

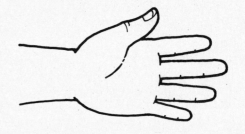

_____

5. How many cans are there in 2 packs?

_____

6. How many legs are there on 2 stools?

_____

Name _____

Ringing Sums

Dear Family,
Our class has just completed a lesson on sums of 10. See how many sums for a given number your child can ring. Observe and listen while your child completes the page.

1. Ring sums of 8.
Tell what you ring.

| 5 | 3 | 4 | 6 |
| 3 | 4 | 4 | 2 |

2. Ring sums of 10.
Tell what you ring.

| 9 | 1 | 8 | 3 |
| 4 | 6 | 2 | 7 |

3. Ring sums of 9.
Tell what you ring.

| 8 | 1 | 6 | 2 |
| 5 | 4 | 3 | 7 |

Name _____

Name That Rule

Work with a partner.

Use a 🖩 to add. Look for a pattern in the sums.

Tell the rule for the pattern.

1.
$$\begin{array}{r} 5 \\ +5 \\ \hline \end{array} \qquad \begin{array}{r} 6 \\ +6 \\ \hline \end{array} \qquad \begin{array}{r} 7 \\ +7 \\ \hline \end{array} \qquad \begin{array}{r} 8 \\ +8 \\ \hline \end{array} \qquad \begin{array}{r} 9 \\ +9 \\ \hline \end{array}$$

Rule: _____

2.
$$\begin{array}{r} 1 \\ +2 \\ \hline \end{array} \qquad \begin{array}{r} 2 \\ +4 \\ \hline \end{array} \qquad \begin{array}{r} 3 \\ +6 \\ \hline \end{array} \qquad \begin{array}{r} 4 \\ +8 \\ \hline \end{array} \qquad \begin{array}{r} 5 \\ +10 \\ \hline \end{array}$$

Rule: _____

3.
$$\begin{array}{r} 9 \\ +0 \\ \hline \end{array} \qquad \begin{array}{r} 8 \\ +2 \\ \hline \end{array} \qquad \begin{array}{r} 7 \\ +4 \\ \hline \end{array} \qquad \begin{array}{r} 6 \\ +6 \\ \hline \end{array} \qquad \begin{array}{r} 5 \\ +8 \\ \hline \end{array}$$

Rule: _____

Do you see any other patterns?
Tell your partner.

Number Stories

Work with a partner.
Ring two groups of things in each set.
Write a number sentence to match.
Take turns telling a story about the number sentence.

1.

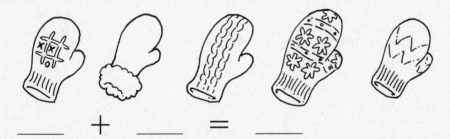

____ + ____ = ____

2.

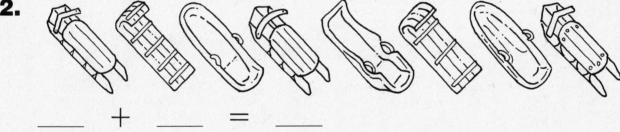

____ + ____ = ____

3.

____ + ____ = ____

4.

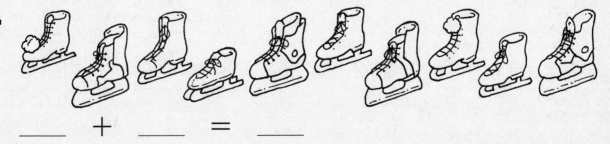

____ + ____ = ____

Math Bingo

Play with a partner.
Take turns spinning a number.
Color a square on your
game board that names
that sum.
Say "Bingo!" when all your
squares are colored.

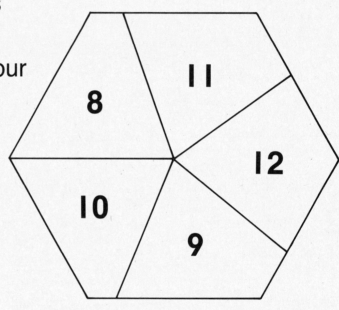

Player 1

6 + 4	5 + 5	5 + 3
5 + 4	9 + 3	6 + 6
4 + 4	5 + 6	7 + 3
6 + 3	6 + 5	4 + 5

Player 2

4 + 5	8 + 3	4 + 4
6 + 5	7 + 3	5 + 6
6 + 6	5 + 4	4 + 6
3 + 5	5 + 5	7 + 2

Name _____

Riddles

Write a number to answer the riddle.

1.
Double me and add 1 to get 7.

Who am I? 3

2.
Double me and add 1 to get 9.

Who am I? ____

3.
Add me to 7 and get 9.

Who am I? ____

4.
Add me to 8 and get 11.

Who am I? ____

5.
Double me and add 2 to get 6.

Who am I? ____

6.
Add me to 4 and get 12.

Who am I? ____

7.
Add me to 3 and get 9.

Who am I? ____

8.
Double me and add 1 to get 11.

Who am I? ____

Name _____

Find the Sums

Ring pairs of numbers side by side
that give the sum shown below.

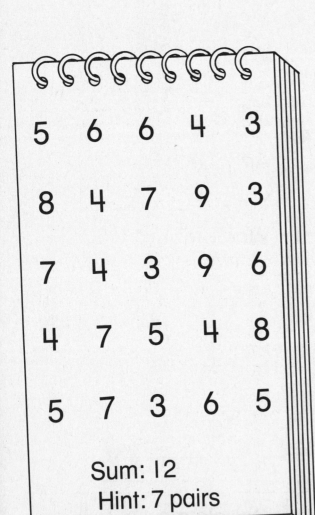

Pad 1:
5	6	6	4	3
8	4	7	9	3
7	4	3	9	6
4	7	5	4	8
5	7	3	6	5

Sum: 12
Hint: 7 pairs

Pad 2:
4	6	8	4	7
7	6	5	2	9
8	4	5	5	6
3	8	9	2	7
6	3	7	4	9

Sum: 11
Hint: 7 pairs

Name _____

Set Sums

Color **3** sets to get the sum.

1. sum

6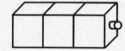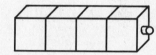

2.

9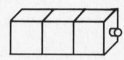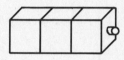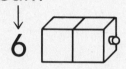

3.

7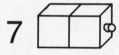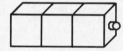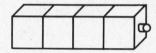

4.

10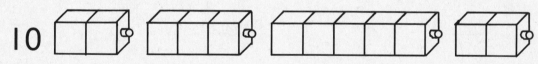

5.

8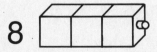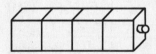

Name _____

Finish the Picture

Finish the picture to show the data.
Then answer the questions.

Each house has 4 .

Each tree has 5 .

Each path has 3 .

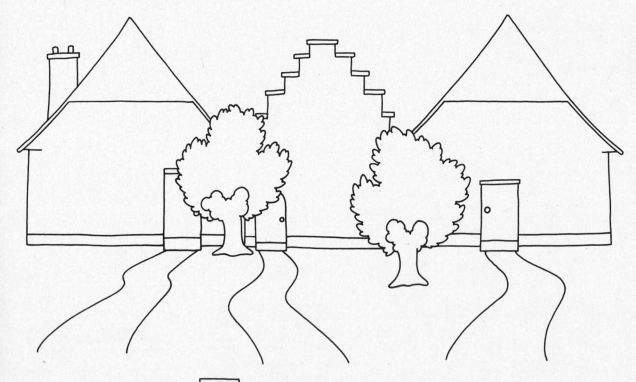

1. How many in all? _____

2. How many in all? _____

3. How many in all? _____

Name _____

Measure Each Other

Work with a partner.
Use string ⌇, scissors ✂,
and paper clips ⌒⌒⌒⌒ .
Estimate and measure lengths on your partner.

1. Measure with string.
   Cut the string.

2. Estimate how many ⌒
   long the string is.
   Write your estimate.

3. Use ⌒ to measure
   the string.
   Write the measure.

Your Partner's	Estimate	Measure
Hand	_____ ⌒	_____ ⌒
Foot	_____ ⌒	_____ ⌒
Neck	_____ ⌒	_____ ⌒
Ear	_____ ⌒	_____ ⌒

Name _____

Inching Along

Dear Family,
   Our class is learning to estimate and measure length in inches. Help your child to find objects around the house and observe as he or she estimates and then measures each one.

Work with a family member. Cut out the inch strip.
Find 3 things in your house to measure. You could
measure a 🍞 , a 📻 , or a 📻 .
Draw a picture of each thing you will measure.
Estimate how many inches. Then measure.

1.

estimate _____ inches

measure _____ inches

2.

estimate _____ inches

measure _____ inches

3.

estimate _____ inches

measure _____ inches

Talk about what you did.

inch	inch	inch	inch	inch	inch

Name _____

Drawing with a Ruler

Use your punchout inch ruler.
Draw the object.

1. A  4 inches long

2. A 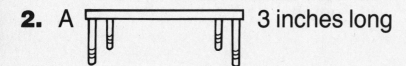 3 inches long

3. A 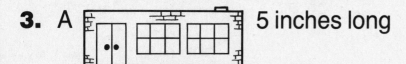 5 inches long

Name _____

Take a Giant Step

Work in groups of 3.
Use a foot ruler and chalk.

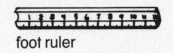
foot ruler

1. Take a giant step. Measure the step you took.

_____ about _____
name

_____ about _____
name

_____ about _____
name

2. Jump. Measure how long.

_____ about _____
name

_____ about _____
name

_____ about _____
name

Name _____

The Long and Short of It

Dear Family,
In our class we are learning how to order by height and length. After your child finds and pastes pictures on the page, encourage discussion as he or she orders the items from shortest to longest. Follow up by having your child arrange the members of your family in a line from shortest to tallest.

Work with a family member.
Look through magazines.
Find 3 pictures that are longer or shorter than the string next to **A**.
Cut them out. Paste them next to **B**, **C**, and **D**.

A.

B.

C.

D.

1. Which is the longest? _____

2. Which is the shortest? _____

3. Which is in between? _____

Name _____

Around the Park

Use an inch ruler to help answer the questions.

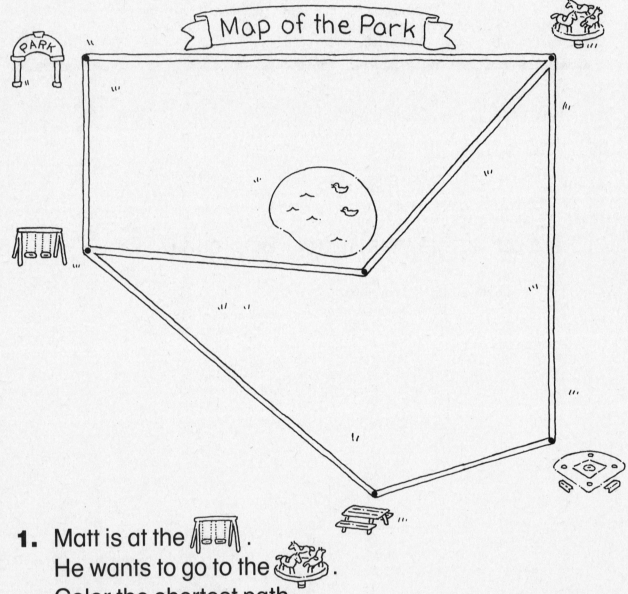

Map of the Park

1. Matt is at the swing.
   He wants to go to the carousel.
   Color the shortest path.

2. Pat is at the baseball field.
   She wants to go to the PARK entrance.
   Color the shortest path.

Name _____

Pathways in the Park

1. Use your punchout centimeter ruler.
Measure the length of each path.
Then write how long in all.

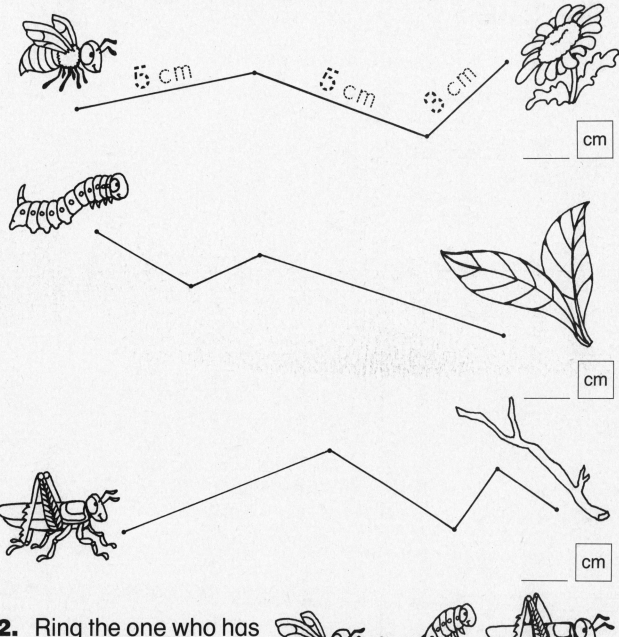

_____ cm

_____ cm

_____ cm

2. Ring the one who has the longest path.

Name _____

Shaping Up

Use your punchout centimeter ruler.
Measure each side. Add the lengths on a 🖩 .
Mark an X inside each shape that measures more than
2 decimeters around.

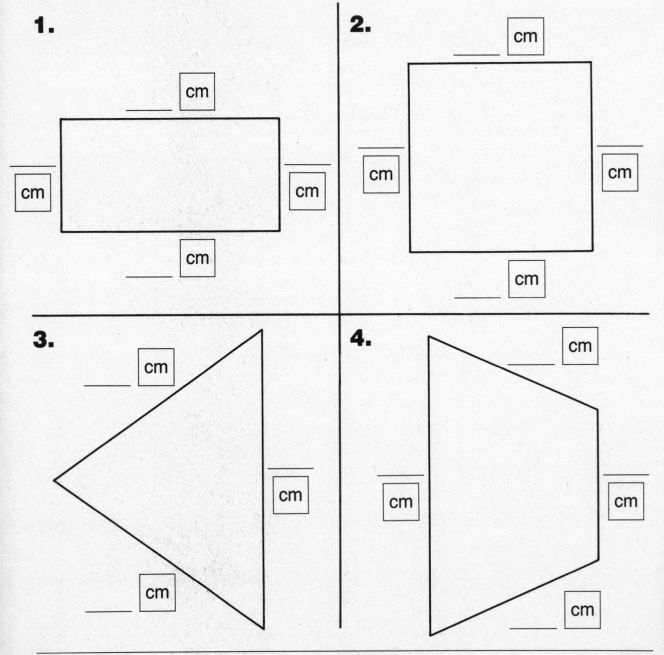

1.

2.

3.

4.

Some Weighty Matters

Draw in enough apples to show the heavier side.

1.

2.

3.

4.

5.

6.

Name _____

Party Time

Draw pictures to help solve the problem.

1. Andy counted 5 red 🎈.
There are 3 fewer blue 🎈
than red 🎈.
There are 2 more yellow 🎈
than blue 🎈.
How many 🎈 are there?

_____ 🎈

2. Maria counted 3 green 🎉.
There is 1 more orange 🎉
than green 🎉.
There are 2 fewer purple 🎉
than orange 🎉.
How many 🎉 are there?

_____ 🎉

Name _____

Find the Missing Number

What number was subtracted, 1 or 2?

1.

$$8 - \boxed{} = 7$$

$$5 - \boxed{} = 3$$

$$11 - \boxed{} = 9$$

$$7 - \boxed{} = 6$$

2.

$$9 - \boxed{} = 7$$

$$6 - \boxed{} = 5$$

$$10 - \boxed{} = 8$$

$$4 - \boxed{} = 3$$

3.

$$3 - \boxed{} = 1$$

$$5 - \boxed{} = 4$$

$$8 - \boxed{} = 6$$

$$6 - \boxed{} = 4$$

4.

$$7 - \boxed{} = 5$$

$$10 - \boxed{} = 9$$

$$4 - \boxed{} = 2$$

$$9 - \boxed{} = 8$$

Name _____

Animal Fun

Use your 🖩 to find how many are left.

1. Press | **5** | for 🐦 in all.

Press | **−** | **1** | **=** | for each 🐦 flying away.

_____ 🐦 are left.

2. | **6** | 🐸 in all. _____ 🐸 are left.

3. | **7** | 🦆 in all. _____ 🦆 are left.

4. | **5** | 🐢 in all. _____ 🐢 are left.

Work with a partner. Take turns telling the stories.

Stepping Stones

Count on or back in your head.
Write the answer.

1. $10 - 2 + 1 - 2 = \bigcirc$

2. $8 + 3 - 3 + 2 = \bigcirc$

3. $12 - 3 - 3 + 1 = \bigcirc$

4. $6 + 2 + 3 - 2 = \bigcirc$

5. $10 - 1 - 2 + 2 = \bigcirc$

Make up a path of your own. Write $+$ or $-$.
Write 1, 2, or 3. Ask a friend to solve.

$9 \quad \bigcirc \quad \bigcirc \quad \bigcirc = \bigcirc$

Name _____

Class Surveys

Use the charts to answer the questions.
Write the number sentence.

1.

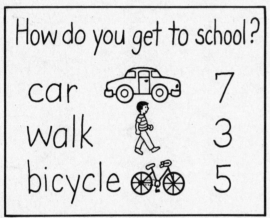

How do you get to school?
car 🚗 7
walk 🚶 3
bicycle 🚲 5

How many more ride a
bicycle than walk?

_____

2.

What pet do you have?
cat 🐱 11
dog 🐕 8
fish 🐟 3

How many more children
have dogs than fish?

_____

3.

What is your favorite sport?

soccer 3

kickball 2

softball 6

How many more picked
softball than kickball?

_____

4.

What is your favorite sandwich?

peanut butter 9

cheese 7

tuna 3

How many more picked
peanut butter than tuna?

_____

Name _____

Follow the Path

Subtract.

Use a red ▭▷ to follow the zero facts.

Help the 🕊 find the 🪺 .

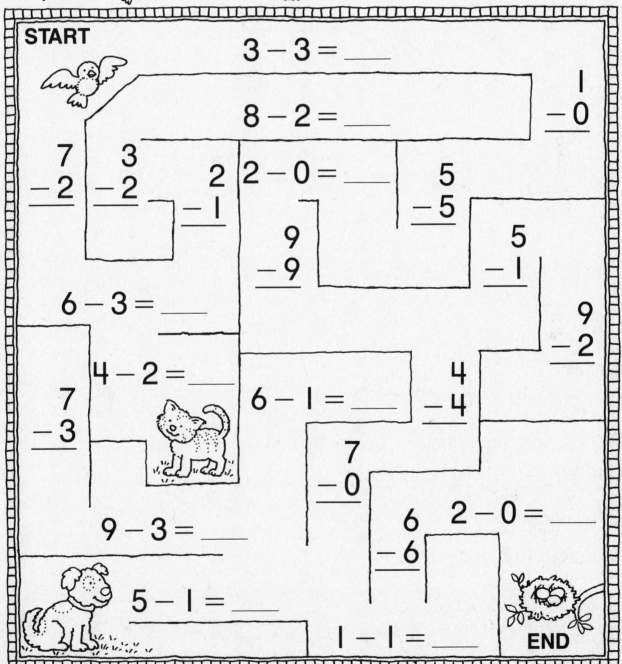

START

$3 - 3 =$ _____

$8 - 2 =$ _____

$\begin{array}{r} 1 \\ -0 \\ \hline \end{array}$

$\begin{array}{r} 7 \\ -2 \\ \hline \end{array}$ $\begin{array}{r} 3 \\ -2 \\ \hline \end{array}$ $\begin{array}{r} 2 \\ -1 \\ \hline \end{array}$ $2 - 0 =$ _____ $\begin{array}{r} 5 \\ -5 \\ \hline \end{array}$

$\begin{array}{r} 9 \\ -9 \\ \hline \end{array}$ $\begin{array}{r} 5 \\ -1 \\ \hline \end{array}$

$6 - 3 =$ _____ $\begin{array}{r} 9 \\ -2 \\ \hline \end{array}$

$4 - 2 =$ _____ $\begin{array}{r} 4 \\ -4 \\ \hline \end{array}$

$\begin{array}{r} 7 \\ -3 \\ \hline \end{array}$ $6 - 1 =$ _____

$\begin{array}{r} 7 \\ -0 \\ \hline \end{array}$

$9 - 3 =$ _____ $\begin{array}{r} 6 \\ -6 \\ \hline \end{array}$ $2 - 0 =$ _____

$5 - 1 =$ _____

$1 - 1 =$ _____ END

Name _____

Patterns

Use your 🖩 to help you.
Write the missing numbers on the keys.
Look for a pattern.

1. [ON/C] [9] [−] [8] [=] [ ] [+] [8] [=] [ ]

2. [ON/C] [9] [−] [6] [=] [ ] [+] [6] [=] [ ]

3. [ON/C] [7] [−] [4] [=] [ ] [+] [4] [=] [ ]

4. [ON/C] [6] [−] [2] [=] [ ] [+] [2] [=] [ ]

5. [ON/C] [5] [−] [0] [=] [ ] [+] [0] [=] [ ]

Write your own numbers on the keys.
Use your 🖩 to help you.

6. [ON/C] [7] [−] [ ] [=] [ ] [+] [ ] [=] [ ]

7. [ON/C] [9] [−] [ ] [=] [ ] [+] [ ] [=] [ ]

Name _____

Double It

Look at the pictures. Find the doubles.
Describe doubles facts and add-to-check facts
to a family member.
Have a family member write the facts.

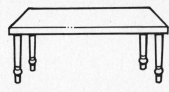

____ − ____ = ____

____ + ____ = ____

____ − ____ = ____

____ + ____ = ____

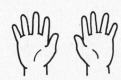

____ − ____ = ____

____ + ____ = ____

____ − ____ = ____

____ + ____ = ____

Find an example of a double. Write the double and
add-to-check fact.

____ − ____ = ____

____ + ____ = ____

Name _____

Number Birds

Dear Family,
    Our class has been learning subtraction facts. Play this game with your child. To prepare for the game, cut a piece of paper into 9 small squares. Number 3 squares 1, 3 squares 2, and 3 squares 3. Put all squares in a cup. Each player will need a marker, such as a button. To play the game, follow these rules.
    Choose a bird. Pick a number square. Move your marker that number of spaces. Answer the subtraction fact on that space aloud. Color in that answer space on your bird. Put the number back in the cup. Now it is the other player's turn. Continue play until both birds are colored. You may have to go around the board more than once.

Play with a family member.

Ask him or her to read the rules aloud.

START

$7-2$ $6-3$ $4-4$ $10-8$

5
-1

8
-2

3
-0

10
-5

9
-9

11
-9

9
-3

7
-7

$10-7$ $7-1$ $7-3$ $8-4$

At the Beach

Work with a partner.

Take turns telling stories about the picture.

Finish your partner's story with a question.

Write the addition or subtraction sentence that matches.

1. the 🧒👧 story

2. the 🏰 story

3. the 🦆 story

4. the ⭐ story

Name _____

Solid Search

Find things in the classroom that have these shapes.
Write the name of the object or
draw a picture of it in the chart.

sphere	cylinder	cube	box

Compare charts with a friend.
Talk about which solids were hard to find.

Solid Search

Dear Family,
  Our class is learning about solids. Help your child find solids at home. Some solids to look for are a video game cartridge, the refrigerator (box); an oatmeal cannister, canned food (cylinder); a birthday hat (cone); a ball (sphere). (For cones, you may need to look for pictures in newspapers and magazines.) Then work on this activity together.

Look for solids in your house.
Draw a picture of each solid you find.
Ask a family member to write the names.

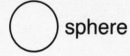 sphere

 cone

 box

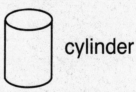 cylinder

Name _____

Who Am I?

Use the picture and the clues to answer the riddle.

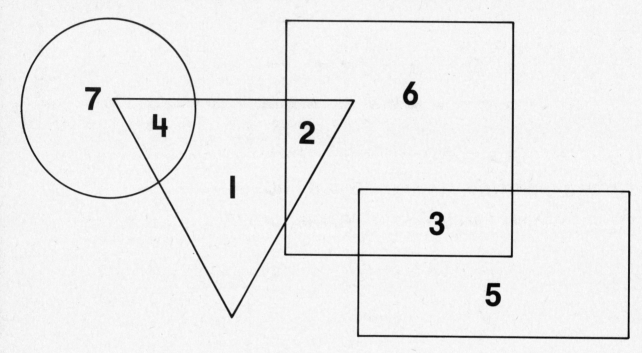

1. I am in the circle.
I am not in the triangle.
What number am I?

_____

2. I am in the triangle.
I am also in the square.
What number am I?.

_____

3. I am in the rectangle.
I am not in the square.
What number am I?

_____

4. I am in the square.
I am not in the triangle.
I am not in the
rectangle.
What number am I?

_____

Figures from Space

Copy Zed and Zap.

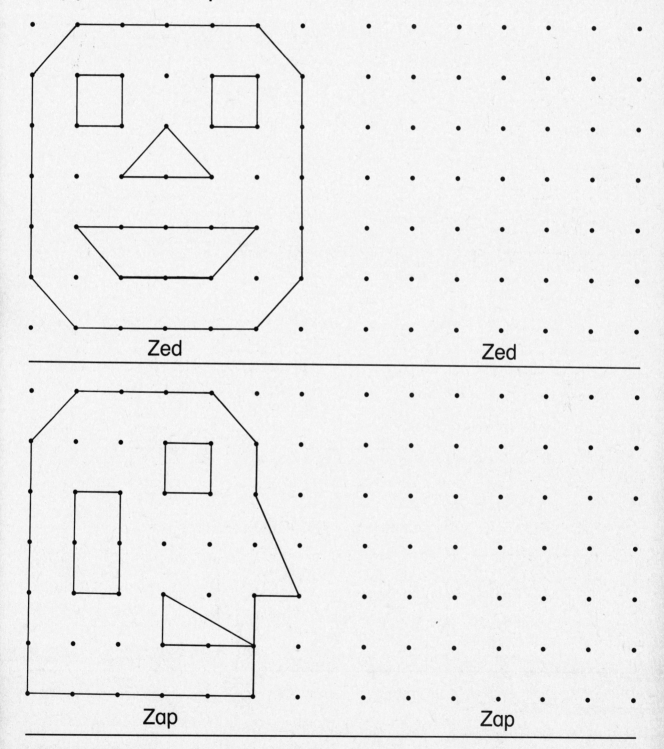

Zed

Zed

Zap

Zap

More than You Think

1. Color a different triangle in each picture.

2. Color a different square in each picture.

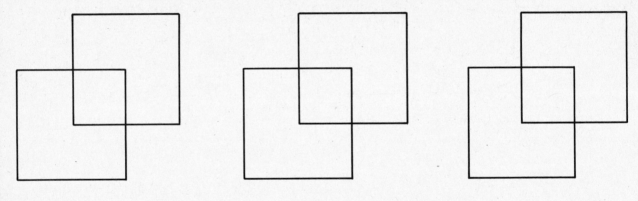

3. Color a different rectangle in each picture.

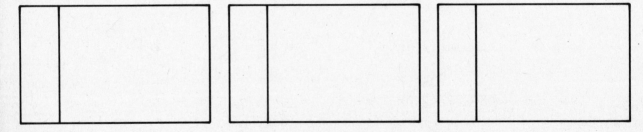

Name _____

What Can I Buy?

Use punchout coins to solve.
Ring **yes** or **no** to answer the question.
Then write how much will be left or
how much more is needed.

flag

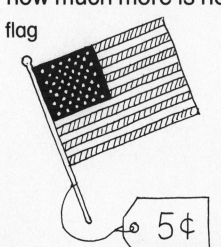  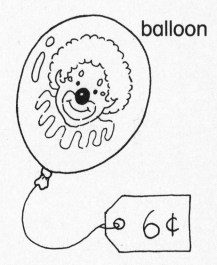

top   balloon

5¢   13¢   6¢

1. I have 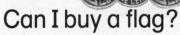 .

Can I buy a flag?   yes   no

I will have ____ ¢ left.   I need ____ ¢ more.

2. I have  .

Can I buy a balloon?   yes   no

I will have ____ ¢ left.   I need ____ ¢ more.

3. I have  .

Can I buy a top?   yes   no

I will have ____ ¢ left.   I need ____ ¢ more.

Name _____

Anything Goes

Make up your own shapes on the geoboard.
Draw them here.
Write how many pegs are inside, outside, and on.

1.

_____ inside

_____ outside

_____ on

2.

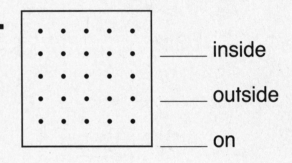

_____ inside

_____ outside

_____ on

3.

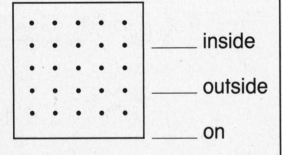

_____ inside

_____ outside

_____ on

4.

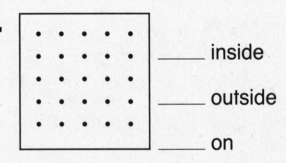

_____ inside

_____ outside

_____ on

Make a Mobile

Dear Family:
    Our class has been working on identifying symmetric figures. Have fun helping your child make a mobile using symmetric figures. You will need paper, scissors, glue, string, and a wire hanger.

Choose a shape or make your own.

Fold two papers in half and draw one part of the shape on each paper. Keep the papers folded and cut out the parts.

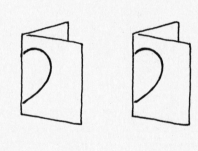

The fold is the line of symmetry. Put glue on each fold line. Glue the figures together with a piece of string at the fold.

Attach the string to the hanger.
Make some more shapes.

Making a Graph

Find figures congruent to those on the graph.
X the figure.

Color a ☐ on the graph.

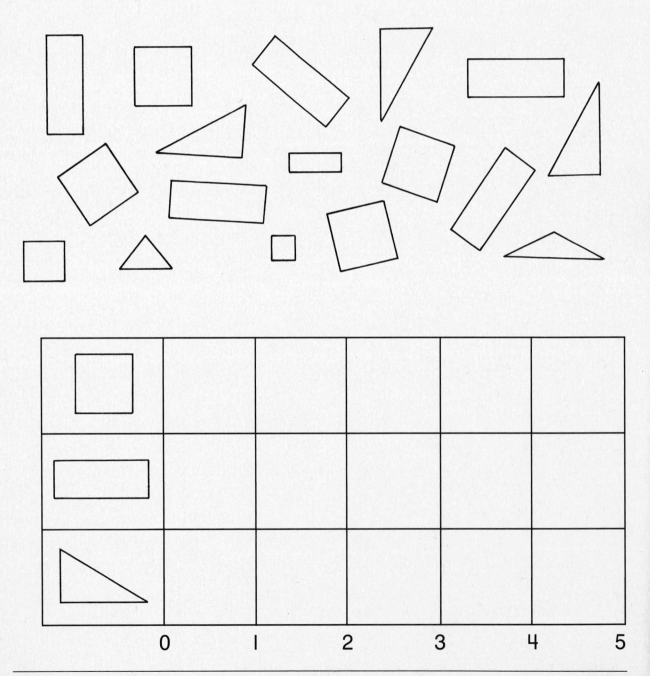

 Use with text pages 195 – 196. **CS-1**

Name _____

Who Lives There?

Use your inch ruler to solve.

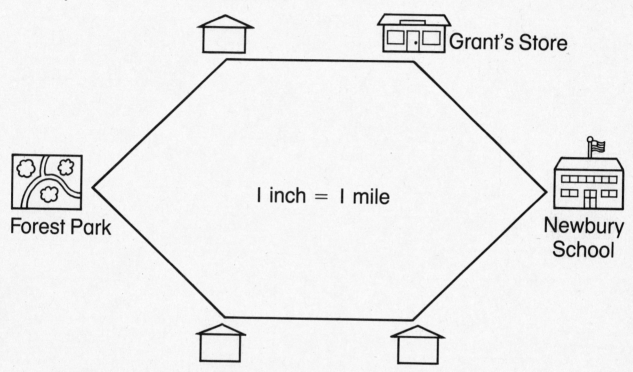

Grant's Store

Forest Park

I inch = I mile

Newbury School

1. Andrea lives 2 miles from Grant's store.
   Write an **A** on her house.

2. Bob lives 4 miles from the park.
   Write a **B** on his house.

3. Clara lives 6 miles from Grant's store.
   Write a **C** on her house.

4. Who lives closest to school? Ring one.

   Andrea   Bob   Clara

5. Who lives closer to the park than the store? Ring one.

   Andrea   Bob   Clara

Name _____

Shape Up

Write the numbers and the number sentence.

1.

	Shapes in All	Take Away	Number Left	Number Sentence
	_____	all ★'s	_____	_____
	_____	all ●'s	_____	_____
	_____	all ■'s	_____	_____
	_____	all ■'s and ●'s	_____	_____

2.

	Shapes in All	Take Away	Number Left	Number Sentence
	_____	all ●'s	_____	_____
	_____	all ▲'s	_____	_____
	_____	all ■'s	_____	_____
	_____	all ★'s	_____	_____
	_____	all ★'s and ▲'s	_____	_____

Name _____

Making Facts

Work in groups of 3.
Use inch graph paper to make
number squares.
Place numbers on your paper
to make facts.
Record your facts.
Compare with friends. Talk about it.

0	5
1	6
2	7
3	8
4	9

$$\begin{array}{r} \square \\ -2 \\ \hline \square \end{array} \qquad \begin{array}{r} \square \\ -7 \\ \hline \square \end{array} \qquad \begin{array}{r} \square \\ -4 \\ \hline \square \end{array}$$

$$\square - 5 = \square$$

$$\square - 1 = \square$$

Name _____

Sticker Sentences

Use the picture to solve.
Write the number sentence and the answer.

Jill's book

Kay's book

1. How many 😊 stickers do Jill and Kay have together?

_____

____ stickers

2. How many more 🤍 stickers does Jill have than Kay?

_____

____ more stickers

3. If Jill gave her ❀ stickers to Kay, how many stickers would she have left?

_____

____ stickers

4. How many more stickers are in Kay's book than Jill's book?

_____

____ more sticker

Name _____

Find All the Ways

Play with a partner.
Take turns.
Use red and yellow counters.
Find 2 outside numbers to
subtract to get the inside number.
Say the fact. Put counters on the numbers.
Cover 4 facts.

9	2	3
0	4	5
4	7	6

$$9 - 5 = 4$$

1.

8	5	2
6	1	7
3	4	9

2.

7	4	10
11	3	2
5	1	8

3.

5	7	1
8	2	10
3	4	6

4.

8	6	3
9	5	4
1	2	7

Name

Follow Your Nose

Add or subtract. End with 12.

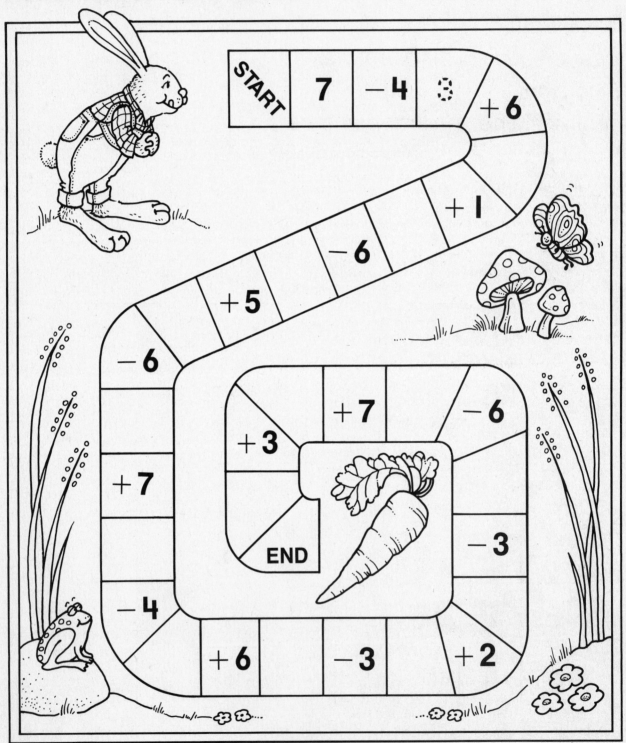

START 7 − 4 3 + 6 + 1 − 6 + 5 − 6 + 3 + 7 − 6 + 7 − 3 − 4 + 6 − 3 + 2 END

Different Facts

Work in groups of 3.
Take turns in each role.

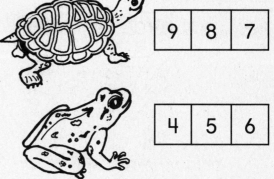

1. One student picks a number from the turtle.

2. One student picks a number from the frog.

3. One student uses those numbers to write a subtraction fact and add-to-check fact.

1.

2.

3.

4.

What Does Not Belong?

Dear Family,
    Our class has been studying fact families. As your child crosses out the fact that does not belong in the family, ask him or her to explain why.

Cross out the fact that does not belong in the family. Finish the other facts.

$6 + 5 =$ ___
$5 + 6 =$ ___
$\cancel{12 - 6} =$ ___
$11 - 6 =$ ___
$11 - 5 =$ ___

$4 + 8 =$ ___
$7 + 5 =$ ___
$5 + 7 =$ ___
$12 - 7 =$ ___
$12 - 5 =$ ___

$4 + 7 =$ ___
$7 + 4 =$ ___
$11 - 4 =$ ___
$11 - 3 =$ ___
$11 - 7 =$ ___

$9 + 3 =$ ___
$3 + 9 =$ ___
$12 - 4 =$ ___
$12 - 9 =$ ___
$12 - 3 =$ ___

Name _____

Color the Last One

Play with a partner. Take turns.

1. Choose a number from 🐟 .

2. Subtract a number from 🐢 .

3. The difference tells you how many 🐸 to color.

4. The person to color the last 🐸 wins.

Name _____

Two Stories in One

Work with a partner.

Each pick a different number for the story.

One partner tells a **joining** story and
writes the addition sentence.

The other partner tells a **how many more**
story and writes the subtraction sentence.

1. ____

____

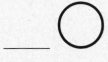

addition story

___ ◯ ___ = ___
in all

subtraction story

___ ◯ ___ = ___
more

2. ____

____

addition story

___ ◯ ___ = ___
in all

subtraction story

___ ◯ ___ = ___
more

Name _____

Look Sharp!

Both boxes have the same number of beads.
Guess and write how many in the first box.
Count and write how many in the second box.

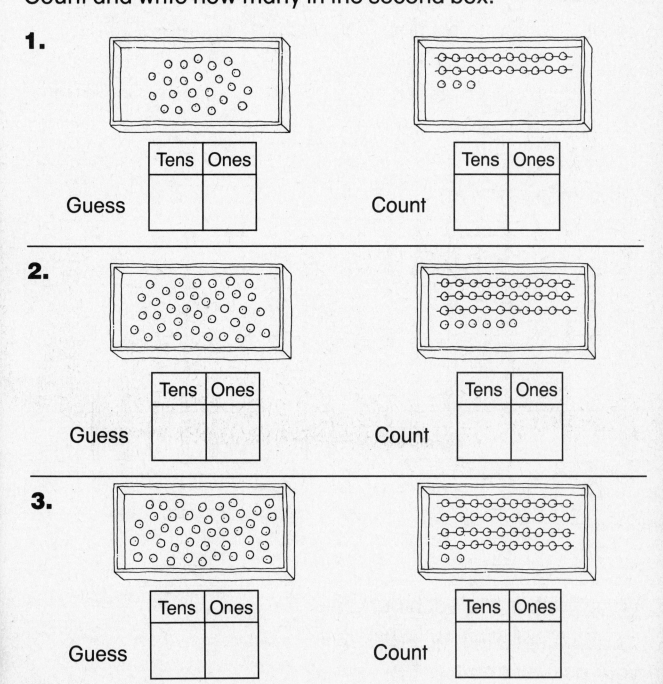

1.

Guess	Tens	Ones

Count	Tens	Ones

2.

Guess	Tens	Ones

Count	Tens	Ones

3.

Guess	Tens	Ones

Count	Tens	Ones

Name _____

Calculator Fun

Work with a partner. Use a .
Enter the first number.
Write what you see.
Enter the second number. Write what you see.

1.

ON/C	4	Tens	Ones
			4
	8	4	8

2.

ON/C	9	Tens	Ones
	9		

3.

ON/C	5	Tens	Ones
	2		

4.

ON/C	8	Tens	Ones
	0		

5.

ON/C	3	Tens	Ones
	7		

6.

ON/C	1	Tens	Ones
	8		

What happens to each number
as you enter it in the ⬚ ? Tell
your partner about it.

Name _____

Count by Tens

Color every **y** [yellow]. Color every **b** [blue].
Color every **g** [green].

How many **y** ☐? ____

How many **g** ◯? ____

How many **b** ☐ and **b** ◯? ____

How many ☐ in all? ____

How many ◯ in all? ____

How many ◯ and ☐ in all? ____

Show and Write

Work in groups of 3.
Use tens and ones models.
Take turns.

1. Show tens and ones in the box.
2. Write how many.
3. Count and check.

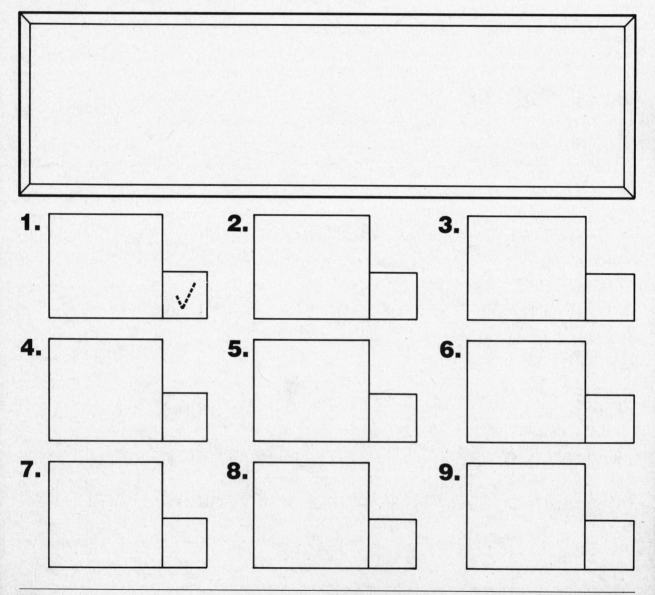

Calculator Counting

Use your . Count on or back.

Press first each time.

1. | 2 | 6 | + | 1 | = | = | = | = | = |

_____

2. | 4 | 5 | + | 1 | = | = | = | = | = |

_____

3. | 1 | 7 | + | 1 | = | = | = | = | = |

_____

4. | 1 | 7 | − | 1 | = | = | = | = | = |

_____

5. | 3 | 4 | − | 1 | = | = | = | = | = |

_____

Name _____

Which Did They Buy?

Add or subtract to solve. Ring the answers.

1. Adam bought 50 marbles.
Which bags did he buy?

 2 tens  1 ten 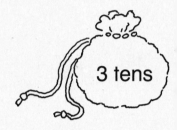 3 tens

2. Julie bought 80 beads.
Which sacks did she buy?

 2 tens 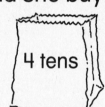 4 tens 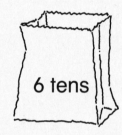 6 tens 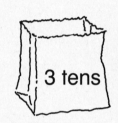 3 tens

3. Simon bought 10 more cherries than strawberries.
Which baskets did he buy?

 3 tens  1 ten  2 tens  4 tens

cherries   cherries   strawberries   strawberries

4. Wendy bought 20 more rocks than shells.
Which bags did she buy?

 6 tens rocks  8 tens rocks  5 tens shells  6 tens shells

Name _____

Shopping

Dear Family,
   Our class is learning how to evaluate groups of dimes and pennies and how to trade pennies for dimes. Please have 50 pennies and 4 dimes on hand for this activity. Play shopping with your child. Observe as he or she counts and trades coins.

A family member chooses something to buy.

The family member pays you with .

You trade as many for as you can.

Write how many.

 27¢   _____ _____

 41¢   _____ _____

 35¢   _____ _____

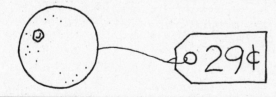 29¢   _____ _____

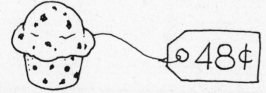 48¢   _____ _____

Adding on the Calculator

Use your to add.

1. (dime) (penny) (penny)   [ON/C] $10 + 1 + 1 =$ _____ ¢

2. (dime) (dime) (dime)   [ON/C] $10 + 10 + 10 =$ _____ ¢

3. (dime) (dime)   [ON/C] $10 + 10 =$ _____ ¢

4. (dime) (dime) (penny)   [ON/C] $10 + 10 + 1 =$ _____ ¢

5. (dime) (penny)   [ON/C] $10 + 1 =$ _____ ¢

Color the answers.

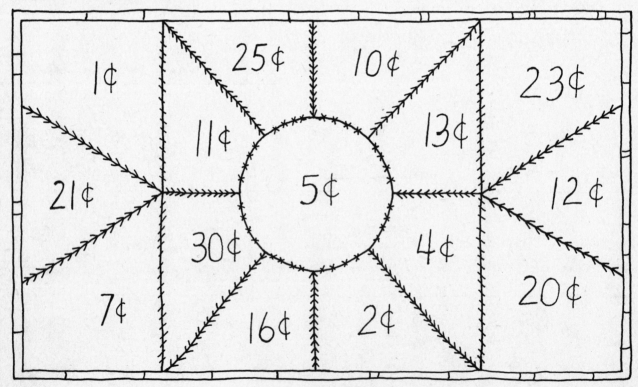

Number Shuffle

Use punchout number cards to solve.

1. Write all the 2-digit numbers you can make with just these cards.

Hint: A card can be used just once to make a number.

5   2   8

___   ___   ___

___   ___   ___

---

2. Write all the 2-digit numbers you can make with just these cards.

3   6   4   9

___   ___   ___

___   ___   ___

___   ___   ___

___   ___   ___

Name _____

Follow the Arrows

1	2	3	4	5	6	7	8	9	10
11	12	13	14	15	16	17	18	19	20
21	22	23	24	25	26	27	28	29→30	
31	32	33	34	35	36	37	38	39	40
41	42	34	44	45	46	47	48	49	50

10 ↓ **20**

29 → **30**

Use the chart. Follow the arrow. Write the new number.

1. 20 ↓ ☐

13 ↓ ☐

36 ↓ ☐

9 ↓ ☐

2. 7 → ☐

26 → ☐

38 → ☐

22 → ☐

3. 6 ↓ → ☐

25 → ↓ ☐

4. 34 → ↓ → ☐

4 ↓ → ↓ ☐

Draw your own arrows. Write the new number in the ☐.

5. 12

6. 23

Name _____

Dots, Dots, Dots

Join the dots. Start at 19.

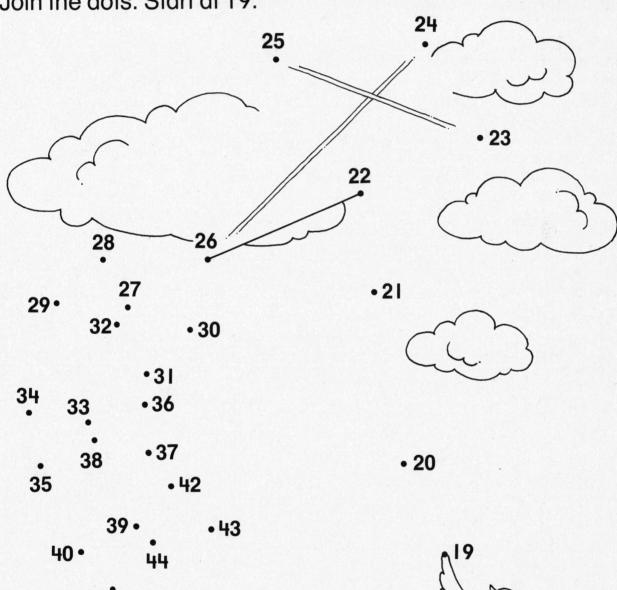

Name _____

Mystery Numbers

Dear Family,
    Our class is learning to count on and back numbers to 100. Help your child master this skill by playing this game. Cover two consecutive numbers with buttons or coins. Ask your child to count forward and backward and say the hidden numbers, then uncover the numbers to check. After a few rounds, you may cover three or more numbers.

1	2	3	4	5	6	7	8	9	10
11	12	13	14	15	16	17	18	19	20
21	22	23	24	25	26	27	28	29	30
31	32	33	34	35	36	37	38	39	40
41	42	43	44	45	46	47	48	49	50
51	52	53	54	55	56	57	58	59	60
61	62	63	64	65	66	67	68	69	70
71	72	73	74	75	76	77	78	79	80
81	82	83	84	85	86	87	88	89	90
91	92	93	94	95	96	97	98	99	100

Name _____

Find the Message

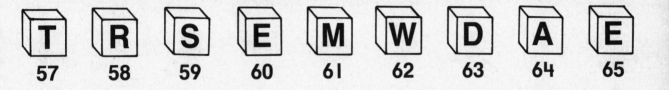

T	R	S	E	M	W	D	A	E
57	58	59	60	61	62	63	64	65

Find the block.
Fill in the letter.
Read the message.

S
just
before
60

just
after
61

just
after
59

just
after
64

just
before
58

between
62 and 64

between
57 and 59

just
before
61

just
after
63

just
before
62

2-Digits and 2 Numbers

Write two 2-digit numbers for each pair of cards. Ring the number that shows more.

8 tens   6 ones   6 tens   8 ones

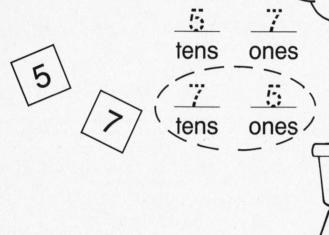

5

7

5 tens   7 ones

(7 tens   5 ones)

1.

2   5

_____ tens   _____ ones

_____ tens   _____ ones

2.

4   3

_____ tens   _____ ones

_____ tens   _____ ones

3.

9   4

_____ tens   _____ ones

_____ tens   _____ ones

4.

5   6

_____ tens   _____ ones

_____ tens   _____ ones

Name _____

How Much More?

Use mental math to solve.

1. Tim has 5 dimes.
Jason has 3 dimes.
How much more money
does Tim have?

_____ ¢ more

2. Marcia has 4 dimes.
Cathy has 1 dime.
How much more money
does Marcia have?

_____ ¢ more

3. Greg has 7 dimes.
Pat has 3 dimes.
How much more money
does Greg have?

_____ ¢ more

4. Reesa has 8 dimes.
Steve had 6 dimes.
How much more money
does Ressa have?

_____ ¢ more

5. Kirsten has 5 dimes.
Josh has 8 dimes.
How much more money
does Josh have?

_____ ¢ more

6. Adam has 4 dimes.
Vera had 9 dimes.
How much more money
does Vera have?

_____ ¢ more

Name _____

Ten More

Work with a partner.
Take turns.
Toss 2 number cubes.
Write a number.
Write the number that is ten more.

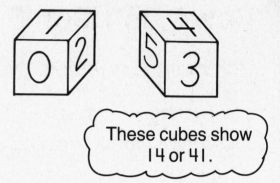

These cubes show 14 or 41.

1. Number   Ten
    Tossed   More

☐ ☐

2. Number   Ten
    Tossed   More

☐ ☐

3. Number   Ten
    Tossed   More

☐ ☐

4. Number   Ten
    Tossed   More

☐ ☐

5. Number   Ten
    Tossed   More

☐ ☐

6. Number   Ten
    Tossed   More

☐ ☐

Name _____

Count by What?

Complete each row. Look for the pattern.

2, 4, 6, 8, □, □, □, □, □

10, 20, 30, 40, □, □, □, □, □

5, 10, 15, 20, □, □, □, □, □

5, 15, 25, 35, □, □, □, □, □

11, 21, 31, 41, 51, □, □, 81, □

0, 3, 6, 9, 12, □, □, 21, □

1, 3, 5, 7, 9, □, □, 15, □

Name _____

Color the Cars

Color the first, fourth, and seventh cars blue.
Color the second, sixth, and eighth cars red.
Color the third, fifth, and ninth cars yellow.

Draw lines to match.

second
fourth
first
third
sixth
seventh
fifth
ninth
eighth

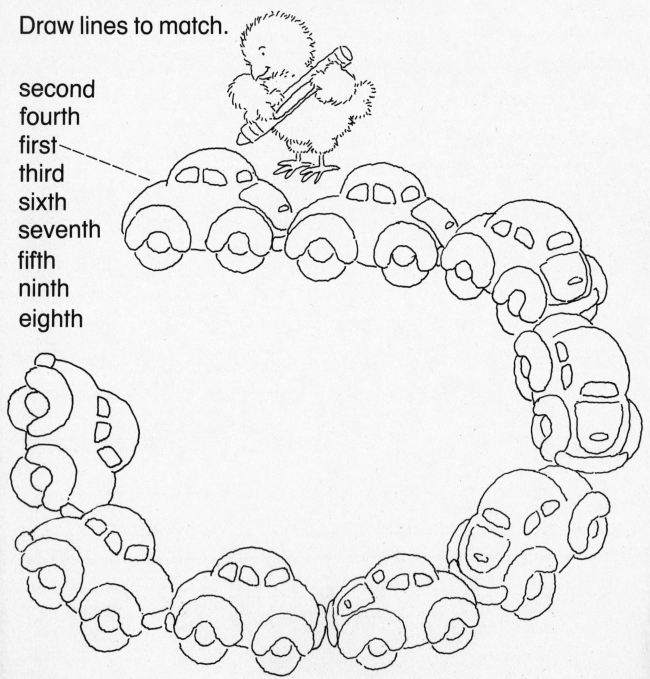

Name _____

Collections

Read each story.
Write the number sentence and the answer for each question.
Then underline the extra data.

1. Amy has 6 stuffed bears.
She has 2 stuffed elephants.
4 of the bears are brown.

How many stuffed animals does Amy have?

_____   _____ stuffed animals

How many more bears than elephants does she have?

_____   _____ more bears

---

2. Paul had 6 coins.
He had 10 stamps. 5 stamps had flower pictures.
Paul gave 3 stamps to his brother.

How many stamps did not have flower pictures?

_____   _____ stamps

How many stamps does Paul have left?

_____   _____ stamps

Can You Buy It?

1. You have

Can you buy 🖊 35¢ ?

(yes)   no

2. You have

Can you buy 🚗 30¢ ?

yes   no

3. You have

Can you buy ✈️ 42¢ ?

yes   no

4. You have

Can you buy 💍 19¢ ?

yes   no

5. You have

Can you buy 🪆 44¢ ?

yes   no

6. You have

Can you buy ⚾ 50¢ ?

yes   no

Name _____

Going Shopping

Buy the fruit. How much do you have left?

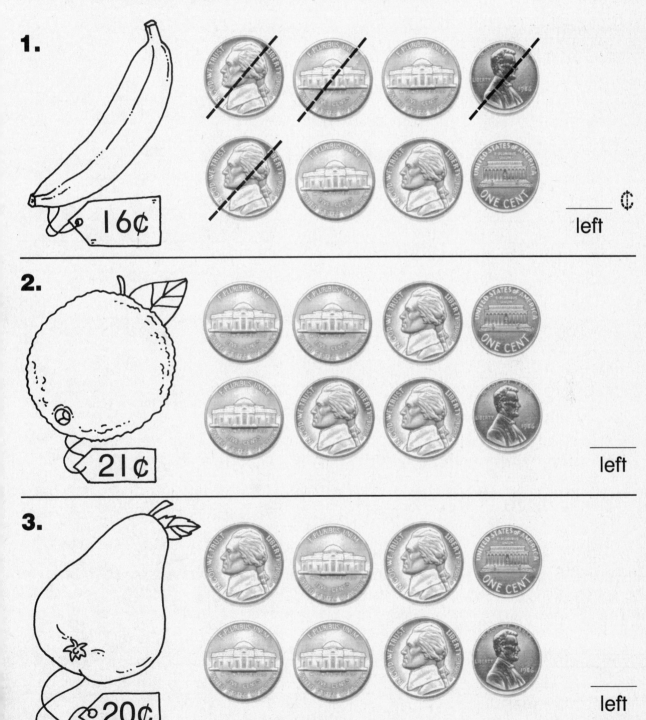

1.

16¢

_____ ¢
left

2.

21¢

_____
left

3.

20¢

_____
left

Name _____

At the Fair

Meg and Lee went to the fair.
Each girl had 50¢ to spend.
Read the story.
Draw an X on the coins the girls spent.

Meg

Meg bought a drink for 10¢.
Meg paid 25¢ for a book.

Lee

Lee bought an apple for 15¢.
Lee paid 10¢ for a pen.

Ring what Meg can buy with the money she has left.
Draw an X on what Lee can buy with the money she has left.

 30¢ 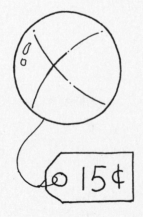 15¢  25¢  45¢

Use with text pages 275–276.

Name _____

Pay the Price

Dear Family,
    Our class has been learning how to count dimes, nickels, and pennies. To help your child do this activity, please provide 9 dimes, 9 nickels, and 9 pennies. Collect grocery items with prices less than 1 dollar. Have your child read the price and count coins to show how to pay the exact amount. Have him or her draw a picture of the object, write the price, and draw the coins.

Draw a picture.   Write the price.   Draw the coins.

Money Maze

Find the path that has the most money.
Draw a red line on the path.
Write the amount in the piggy bank.

Name _____

Money Problems

Add or subtract to solve. Write the answer.

1. Sue has 🪙🪙🪙🪙 .
Rita has 4¢.
How much do they have together?

They have ____ ¢.

2. Carl has 🪙🪙🪙 .
Andy has 6¢.
How much more does Carl have?

Carl has ____ ¢ more.

3. Will had 🪙🪙🪙 .
He spent 7¢.
How much does Will have now?

Will has ____ ¢.

4. Maria had 🪙🪙🪙🪙 .
She earned 3¢ more.
How much does Maria have now?

Maria has ____ ¢.

Name _____

A Money Game

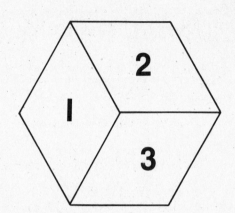

Play with a partner. Use punchout
counters and coins.

Each player starts with

2 , 3 , 3 , 5 .

Put 3 and 5 in a paper cup for the bank.

Take turns. Spin. Move your counter that number
of spaces. Play until both reach **End**.
Then count your money and tell your total.

Start	Give 5¢ to partner.	→ Go ahead 3 □s.	Take 1¢ from partner.
			Put 25¢ in bank.
↓ Go ahead 2 □s.	Take 17¢ from partner.	Give 10¢ to partner.	Take 25¢ from bank.
Go back 3 □s. ↑			
Put 21¢ in bank.	Take 35¢ from bank.	← Go back 2 □s.	**End**

Name _____

What Could You Buy?

Dear Family,
Your child is learning to solve problems using data from newspaper ads. Help your child find some food ads in the newspaper. Ask your child to cut out the pictures and prices. Then help him or her fill in the chart below and solve the problems.

Write the food names and prices here.

Food Name	Price

1. If you had  , what could you buy?

_____

2. If you had  , what could you buy?

_____

3. If you had  , what could you buy?

_____

Name _____

Hands Off

Can you tell the time just by looking at the hands?

1. _____ o'clock

2. _____ o'clock

3. _____ o'clock

4. _____ o'clock

5. _____ o'clock

6. _____ o'clock

Name _____

Watch the Clock

Dear Family,
  Circle a clock in each row. Then have your child read aloud the time on that clock and circle the other clock in the row that shows the same time. For the last row, name a time on the hour and have your child show that time on both clocks. Help your child to read both analog and digital clocks at home when they are on the hour.

Ask a family member to ring a clock.
Ring a clock that shows the same time.

1.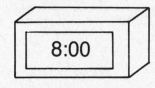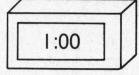

2.

3.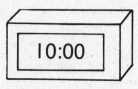

4. Make these clocks show the same time.

 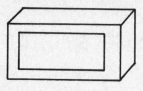

Name _____

How Long?

Solve. Write the answer.

1. Chris read his book from

  to  .

How long did he read? _____ hour

2. Jody played ball from

 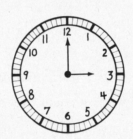 to 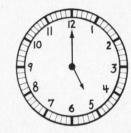 .

How long did she play? _____ hours

3. Sal slept from

  to  .

How long did he sleep? _____ hours

Name _____

Tick-Tack-Tock

Player 1 has 8 yellow counters.

Player 2 has 8 red counters.

Take turns. Read aloud the time on a clock.

Show the same time on your punchout clock.

Put one of your counters on the clock.

Try to get 4 counters in a row →,

or 4 counters in a column ↓.

Where Are You?

Dear Family,
    Our class has been learning how to tell time to the hour and half hour. Write a number in each sentence to show a time on the hour in Exercise 1, and a time on the half hour in Exercise 2. Have your child draw the hands on the clock to show the time, then tell what he or she usually does at that time. Complete the sentence by writing what your child says. Then ask your child to draw a picture that shows the activity. You may wish to talk about daily routines and things that happen at the same time every day.

1. Where are you at _____ o'clock in the morning?
Draw the hands on the clock. Then draw a picture.

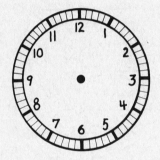

I am _____.

2. Where are you at _____ at night?
Draw the hands on the clock. Then draw a picture.

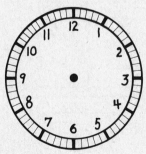

I am _____.

Name _____

Which Month?

Answer the questions. Think about which month it could be.

Sunday	Monday	Tuesday	Wednesday	Thursday	Friday	Saturday

1. This month has 30 days.
Write the dates on the calendar. _____

2. What day is the last day
of this month? _____

3. Flag Day is the second Sunday. What is the date? _____

4. This month comes just after May.
Write the name of this month on the calendar. _____

5. School ends on the fourth Friday.
Write the month and the date. _____

Name _____

Zoo Time

Use the chart to help solve.
Ring your answers.

Feeding Times

Animal	Time
monkeys	10:00
lions	10:30
elephants	11:00
bears	12:00
zebras	1:30
giraffes	2:30

1. If Amy goes to the zoo from ⟦12:00⟧ to ⟦2:00⟧,
which animals can she see being fed?

elephants   bears   zebras   giraffes

2. If Raul goes to the zoo from ⟦10:30⟧ to ⟦11:30⟧,
which animals can he see being fed?

monkey   lions   bears   elephants

3. If Alison goes to the zoo from ⟦1:30⟧ to ⟦3:00⟧,
which animals can she see being fed?

zebras   bears   elephants   giraffes

Nine and Ten Pattern

Color beads to show the number in the △.
Write the missing number. Write the sum.

1.

$9 \quad + \quad \boxed{4}^{\triangle} \quad = \quad 10 \quad + \quad \underline{} \quad = \quad \square$

2.

$9 \quad + \quad \boxed{6}^{\triangle} \quad = \quad 10 \quad + \quad \underline{} \quad = \quad \square$

3.

$7 \quad + \quad \boxed{9}^{\triangle} \quad = \quad 10 \quad + \quad \underline{} \quad = \quad \square$

4.

$5 \quad + \quad \boxed{9}^{\triangle} \quad = \quad 10 \quad + \quad \underline{} \quad = \quad \square$

Name _____

Double the Fun

Use a number from 1 to 9 to answer these double riddles.

1.
Double me and get 12.

Who am I? _____

2.
My double is 8.

Who am I? _____

3.
Double me and get 16.

Who am I? _____

4.
My double is between 4 and 8.

Who am I? _____

5.
My double is less than 4.

Who am I? _____

6.
My double has 2 digits.
One of them is 0.
I am less than 9.

Who am I? _____

7.
My double is between 12 and 16.

Who am I? _____

8.
My double is more than 16.

Who am I? _____

The Adding Game

Play with a partner.
Each player uses a red or yellow counter.
Take turns. Toss a number cube.
Move a counter that many squares.
Add the numbers on the square.
Color the sum at the bottom red or yellow.
Play until all sums are colored.

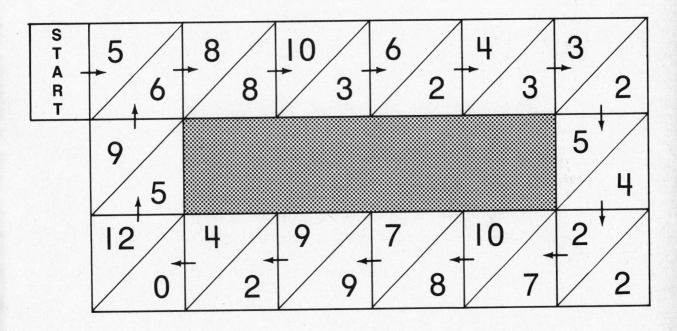

Sums

12	8	18	6	11	14	17
4	16	9	15	7	5	13

Name _____

Kangaroo Hop

Dear Family,
   Our class is learning to add three numbers. To help your child practice, work with him or her on the following activity. Provide 18 counting objects, such as buttons or beans. Have your child make a pile to show the sum, take out the numbers given, and count to find the number that is left, the missing number. Ask your child to count aloud as you listen.

Use counters to find the missing number.

1. $4 + 4 + \bigcirc = 12$

2. $6 + 3 + \bigcirc = 14$

3. $2 + 2 + \bigcirc = 11$

4. $5 + 3 + \bigcirc = 16$

5. $4 + 5 + \bigcirc = 18$

6. $7 + 2 + \bigcirc = 15$

Name _____

Are There Enough?

Ring **Yes** or **No** to answer each question.
If **No**, write how many more are needed.

1. There are 5 bones in the yard.
There are 7 dogs in the yard.
Is there a bone for each dog?

Yes   No   _____ more are needed.

_____

2. There are 9 bananas in the tree.
There are 8 monkeys under the tree.
Is there a banana for each monkey?

Yes   No   _____ more are needed.

_____

3. There are 6 flies on the rock.
There are 10 frogs in the pond.
Is there a fly for each frog?

Yes   No   _____ more are needed.

_____

4. There are 12 horses in the field.
There are 9 carrots.
Is there a carrot for each horse?

Yes   No   _____ more are needed.

_____

Name _____

Seeing Double — Then One

Add.

Match the double to the doubles plus one.

1. $3 + 3 = \underline{6}$ $5 + 6 = \underline{}$

2. $5 + 5 = \underline{}$ $4 + 5 = \underline{}$

3. $8 + 8 = \underline{}$ $3 + 4 = \underline{7}$

4. $4 + 4 = \underline{}$ $8 + 9 = \underline{}$

5. $6 + 6 = \underline{}$ $7 + 8 = \underline{}$

6. $7 + 7 = \underline{}$ $6 + 7 = \underline{}$

Name _____

Eating Well

Dear Family,
   Help your child practice and apply the addition facts we have been studying. Provide 18 pennies or other small objects to represent pennies, such as beans or buttons. Observe as your child solves the problems. Then help him or her make up other problems using the food prices. Write the problems and have your child solve them.

Solve. Use to help.

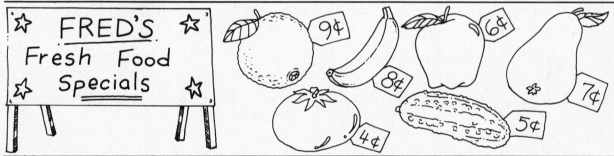

1. John bought a 🍌 and a 🍐. How much money did he spend?

_____

2. Fred sold 2 🍎🍎 to Sam. How much money did they cost in all?

_____

3. Miss Brown bought an 🍎 and a 🍊. How much money did she spend?

_____

4. Tara bought a 🍅, a 🥒, and an 🍊. What was her total?

_____

Now make up some of your own.

Name _____

Secret Numbers

Read the directions. Find the number.
Use the space to write if you need to.

---

1. Start with 2.
Double it.
Add 9.
What is the number? ____

---

2. Start with 3.
Add 6.
Add 7.
What is the number? ____

---

3. Start with 4.
Double it.
Double the double.
What is the number? ____

---

4. Start with 9.
Subtract 3.
Add 1.
Double the sum.
What is the number? ____

Caps and Shirts

Mary Ann has a blue cap and a red cap.
She also had a yellow shirt and an
orange shirt.

1. Color Mary Ann's caps and shirts.

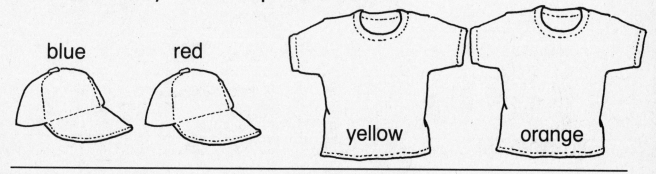

blue   red   yellow   orange

2. Find 4 different ways Mary Ann can
put the colors together.
Color the pictures to show the ways.

Name _____

How Many Are Hiding?

Use counters to help solve.
Write the number.

1.

| 4 birds in all |

How many in the

birdhouse? _____

2.

| 12 bees in all |

How many in the

beehive? _____

3.

| 12 apples in all |

How many in the

bag? _____

4.

| 18 nuts in all |

How many in the

dish? _____

5.

| 14 rocks in all |

How many in the

box? _____

6.

| 16 worms in all |

How many in the

hole? _____

Name _____

Guess and Check

Guess the number. Use a to check.

1. Subtract 9 from me.
The difference is
the same as $11 - 3$.

Who am I? _____

2. Subtract 9 from me.
The difference is
the same as $8 - 2$.

Who am I? _____

3. Subtract 9 from me.
The difference is
the same as $10 - 5$.

Who am I? _____

4. Subtract 9 from me.
The difference is
the same as $7 - 4$.

Who am I? _____

5. Subtract 9 from me.
The difference is
the same as $6 - 2$.

Who am I? _____

6. Subtract 9 from me.
The difference is
the same as $10 - 3$.

Who am I? _____

7. Subtract 9 from me.
The difference is
the same as $11 - 2$.

Who am I? _____

8. Subtract 9 from me.
The difference is
the same as $9 - 7$.

Who am I? _____

Shopping

Solve.

1. Maria has 8¢. How much more money does she need to buy the ✐ ? ____

2. Seth had 15¢. He bought the 🚢 . How much money does he have left? ____

3. Gail has 7¢. How much more money does she need to buy the 📓 ? ____

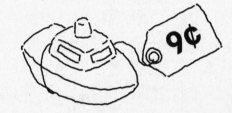

4. Rita has 6¢. Nora has 3¢. They want to buy the 📖 together. How much more money do they need? ____

5. Carl has 12¢. He bought the two ◎ ◎ . How much money does he have left? ____

Name _____

Make up Your Own

Use your own number to finish the story.
Then write a subtraction sentence to solve.

1. 9 children are playing tag.

_____ are boys. The rest are girls.

How many are girls? $9 \ominus$ _____ = _____

_____ girls

2. 11 children are at a pool.

_____ are in the water. The others are not.

How many are not in the water?   _____ $\ominus$ _____ = _____

_____ children

3. 12 children went to the park.

_____ rode bikes. The rest walked.

How many walked?   _____ $\ominus$ _____ = _____

_____ children

4. 10 children are playing catch.

_____ had a turn. The others have not.

How many have not had a turn?   _____ $\ominus$ _____ = _____

_____ children

Creating Facts

Work with a partner. Take turns.

1. Pick a □ number and a ▽ number. Write the addition fact.

2. Use the addition fact to write a subtraction fact.

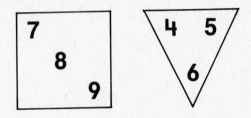

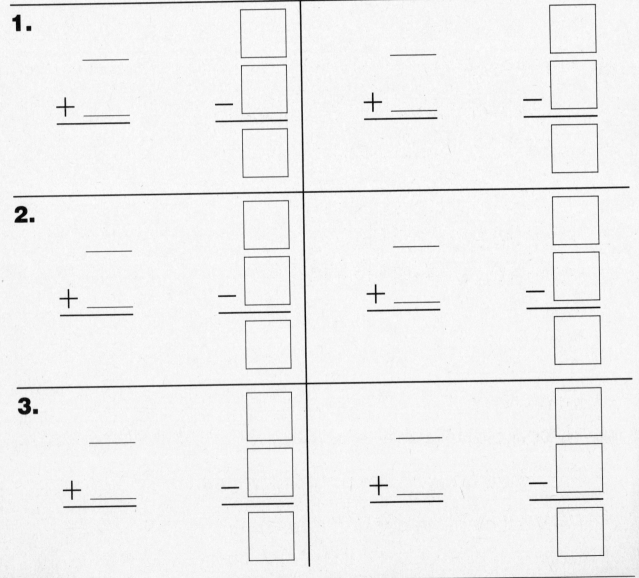

Name _____

Matching Facts

Add. Then subtract. Match the add-to-check fact
to its subtraction fact.

1. $5 + 8 = 13$

2. $8 + 7 = \underline{}$

3. $8 + 8 = \underline{}$

4. $9 + 7 = \underline{}$

5. $6 + 7 = \underline{}$

6. $9 + 9 = \underline{}$

7. $6 + 8 = \underline{}$

8. $7 + 7 = \underline{}$

$16 - 7 = \underline{}$

$16 - 8 = \underline{}$

$13 - 8 = 5$

$15 - 7 = \underline{}$

$18 - 9 = \underline{}$

$13 - 7 = \underline{}$

$14 - 8 = \underline{}$

$14 - 7 = \underline{}$

Name _____

Dear Family,
  Our class has been studying related subtraction facts. Provide your child with a pencil, a large piece of paper folded in half, and 18 small objects to use as counters, such as buttons, paper clips, or toothpicks. Ask your child to talk about the <u>whole</u> number and the <u>parts</u> as he or she does the activity below.

Work with a family member.
Use counters on a piece of paper
to show the parts.
Write the related subtraction facts.

1. Whole $\boxed{13}$

Part $\boxed{7}$ Part $\boxed{6}$

$13 - 6 =$ ____ and

$13 - 7 =$ ____

2. Whole $\boxed{15}$

Part $\boxed{6}$ Part $\boxed{9}$

$15 - 9 =$ ____ and

$15 - 6 =$ ____

3. Whole $\boxed{14}$

Part $\boxed{8}$ Part $\boxed{6}$

$14 - 6 =$ ____ and

$14 - 8 =$ ____

4. Whole $\boxed{16}$

Part $\boxed{9}$ Part $\boxed{7}$

$16 - 7 =$ ____ and

$16 - 9 =$ ____

Part Is Missing

Write the missing part.
Then use the numbers to write four facts.

1.

whole
13

$\underline{}$ $\underline{}$
part part

___ + ___ = ___

___ + ___ = ___

___ − ___ = ___

___ − ___ = ___

2.

whole
15

$\underline{7}$ $\underline{}$
part part

___ + ___ = ___

___ + ___ = ___

___ − ___ = ___

___ − ___ = ___

3.

whole
17

$\underline{8}$ $\underline{}$
part part

___ + ___ = ___

___ + ___ = ___

___ − ___ = ___

___ − ___ = ___

Name _____

In the Garden

Read each story.
Write the number sentence.
Write the answer in a sentence.

1. Lani planted 8 red tulips.
She planted 5 yellow tulips.
How many tulips did she plant in all?

____ ◯ ____ = ____

_____

- -

_____

2. Don had 5 tomato plants.
He had 9 lettuce plants.
How many more lettuce than tomato plants did he have?

____ ◯ ____ = ____

_____

- -

_____

3. Alicia put 12 peaches in a basket.
Then she gave away 3 peaches.
How many peaches are in the basket now?

____ ◯ ____ = ____

_____

- -

_____

Crossnumber Puzzle

Use the **Across** clues to solve.
Use the **Down** clues to check.

Across →

1. $24 + 2$
3. $36 + 1$
5. $81 + 3$
6. $39 + 2$
7. $52 + 3$
9. $59 + 1$
10. $96 + 3$
12. $71 + 2$
14. $19 + 3$
15. $47 + 1$

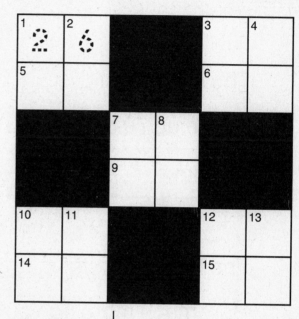

Down ↓

1. $27 + 1$
2. $61 + 3$
3. $32 + 2$
4. $69 + 2$
7. $53 + 3$

8. $48 + 2$
10. $90 + 2$
11. $89 + 3$
12. $73 + 1$
13. $35 + 3$

Name _____

How Much More?

Solve. Use punchout dimes and pennies to help.

1. You have .

The apple costs 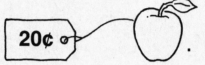 .

How much more do you need? _____ ¢

2. You have .

The orange costs 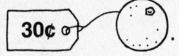 .

How much more do you need? _____ ¢

3. You have .

The plum costs  .

How much more do you need? _____ ¢

3. You have .

The banana costs  .

How much more do you need? _____ ¢

Name _____

The Book Club

Use the graph to answer the questions.

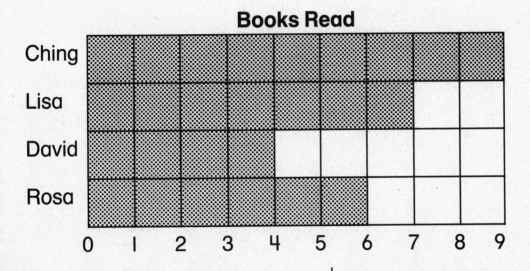

Books Read

1. How many books did Ching and Lisa read in all?

   _____ books

2. How many books did Rosa and David read in all?

   _____ books

3. How many more books did Lisa read than David?

   _____ books

4. How many more books did Ching read than Lisa?

   _____ books

5. How many fewer books did Rosa read than Ching?

   _____ books

6. How many books were read by the children in the club altogether?

   _____ books

Name _____

Counting On By Dimes

Use punchout and . Put coins in
the box to show the first number. Put in
dimes for the second number. Count on by tens.
Write the numbers and the sum.

Coin
 Box

1.
$$13¢$$
$$+20¢$$
$$\overline{}¢$$

13¢
¢
¢

2.
$$57¢$$
$$+10¢$$
$$\overline{}¢$$

57¢
¢

3.
$$29¢$$
$$+30¢$$
$$\overline{}¢$$

29¢
¢
¢
¢

4.
$$42¢$$
$$+30¢$$
$$\overline{}¢$$

¢
¢
¢
¢

5.
$$68¢$$
$$+20¢$$
$$\overline{}¢$$

¢
¢
¢

6.
$$35¢$$
$$+30¢$$
$$\overline{}¢$$

¢
¢
¢
¢

Planning a Picnic

Ring another set to make the sum.

1. 90 cups

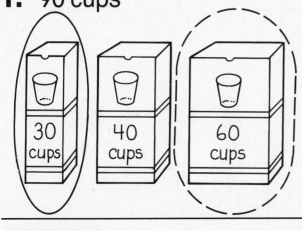

2. 50 forks

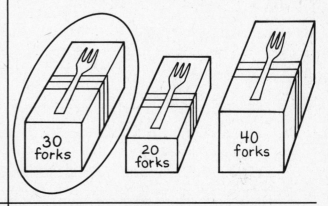

3. 45 bags

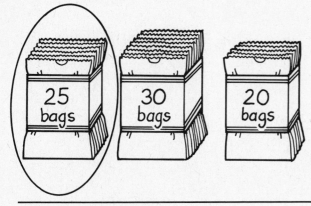

4. 75 plates

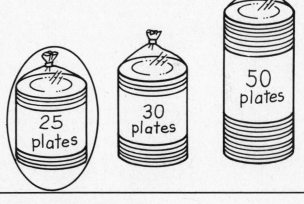

5. 70 straws

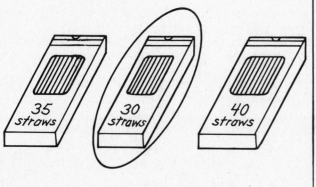

6. 50 spoons

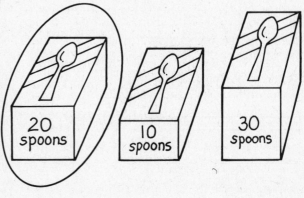

Name _____

Count Back In Your Head

Count back to find the difference.

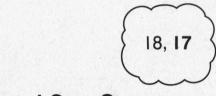
18, 17

1. $19 - 2 = $ ___

2. $23 - 2 = $ ___

3. $27 - 3 = $ ___

4. $18 - 1 = $ ___

5. $29 - 1 = $ ___

6. $24 - 2 = $ ___

7. $32 - 1 = $ ___

8. $36 - 3 = $ ___

9. $38 - 2 = $ ___

10. $37 - 1 = $ ___

11. $15 - 3 = $ ___

12. $26 - 3 = $ ___

13. $35 - 2 = $ ___

14. $38 - 2 = $ ___

Name _____

Try to Get Ahead

Play with a partner.
Use 2 counters and a number cube.
Take turns. Throw the cube and move
that many spaces.

◇ means subtract 10. Move back to the number.

▽ means subtract 20. Move back to the number.

◯ means subtract 30. Move back to the number.

START

10

| 11 | 12 | 13 | 14 | 15 | 16 | 17 | 18 | 19 |

| | | | | | | | | 20 |

| 29 | 28 | 27 | ◇26◇ | 25 | 24 | 23 | ◇22◇ | 21 |

| ◇30◇ |

| 31 | 32 | ▽33▽ | 34 | 35 | ▽36▽ | 37 | ◇38◇ | 39 | ◯40◯ |

FINISH

Name _____

Subtraction Squares

Use a ⬜ .
Subtract across.
Subtract down.
The last box should have the answer for two subtractions.

1.

47	22	25
13	11	

2.

58	35	
26	14	

3.

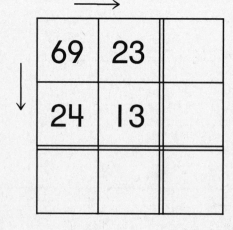

69	23	
24	13	

4.

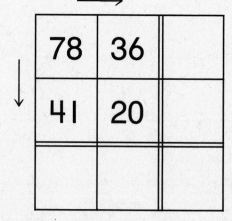

78	36	
41	20	

Name _____

Comparing Methods

Work with a partner.

Each partner picks a different method to solve a problem.

Choose mental math, blocks and paper and pencil,

or a calculator.

Talk about which method was best and why.

1. How much does it cost for both?

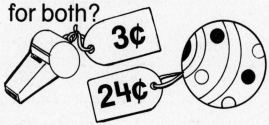

They cost ____ in all.

2. How many tickets did the children sell in all?

Manual	37 tickets
Judy	16 tickets

They sold ____ tickets in all.

3. How many more minutes did Jan practice on Monday than Friday?

Piano Practice	
Monday	45 minutes
Friday	20 minutes

She practiced ____ more minutes on Monday.

4. How many seeds are there in all?

| 22 seeds | 34 seeds | 23 seeds |

There are ____ seeds in all.

Name _____

Draw and Tell

Work with a partner. Take turns.
One draws. The other circles groups of two.
Count together by twos to tell how many in all.
Write the number.

1. Draw ◯. Draw 2 twos.

_____ in all

2. Draw ☐. Draw 5 twos.

_____ in all

3. Draw △. Draw 3 twos.

_____ in all

4. Draw ☐. Draw 4 twos.

_____ in all

Name _____

Groups of Five and Extras

1. Draw 5 ⊘ in each box.

Draw 3 extra ⊘ .

____ ⊘ in all.

2. Draw 5 ✕ in each box.

Draw 2 extra ✕ .

____ ✕ in all.

3. Draw 5 ✐ in the box.

Draw 1 extra ✐ .

____ ✐ in all.

4. Draw 5 △ in each box.

Draw 4 extra △ .

____ △ in all.

What Is Missing?

Write a subtraction sentence to solve each problem.
Write the answer.

1. 12 clowns are at the circus. How many are in the tent?

_____ _____ clowns

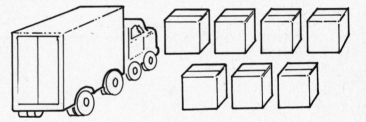

2. There are 15 boxes in all. How many are on the truck?

_____ _____ boxes

3. 11 children are playing. How many are in the clubhouse?

_____ _____ children

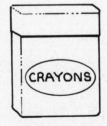

4. Jamie has 16 crayons. How many are in the box?

_____ _____ crayons

Party Fun

Mark has 4 tables for his birthday party.
He puts the same number of things at each table.
He has

16   8   4   16

Draw the things at each table.
Use counters to help decide how many.

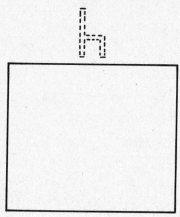

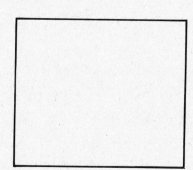

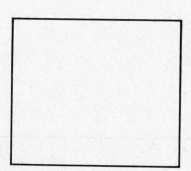

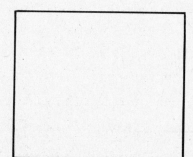

Name _____

Packing Toys

Show the amount of toys.
Make equal groups for each box.
Write how many boxes are full.
Write how many toys are extra.

1. 14 🚗

4 in each box

_____ boxes are full.

_____ 🚗 are extra.

2. 19 🧒

2 in each box

_____ boxes are full.

_____ 🧒 extra.

3. 20 🐊

3 in each box

_____ boxes are full.

_____ 🐊 are extra.

4. 18 🤖

5 in each box

_____ boxes are full.

_____ 🤖 are extra.

Name _____

Make Halves

Draw a line to make halves. Color $\frac{1}{2}$.

1.

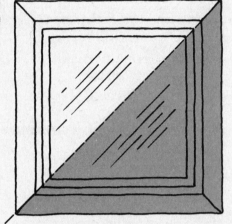

2.

3.

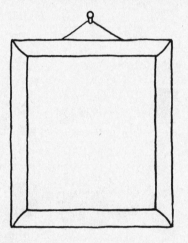

4.

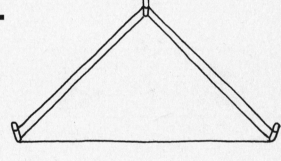

5.

6.

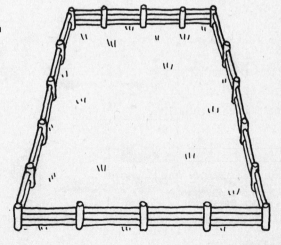

Name _____

Fraction Bingo

Dear Family,
   Our class is studying fractions. Play this game with your child. Make a set of playing cards by writing each of these fractions on 2 index cards: $\frac{1}{2}, \frac{1}{3}, \frac{1}{4}, \frac{2}{3}, \frac{2}{4}$, and $\frac{3}{4}$. Shuffle the cards and place them facedown in a pile. Take turns drawing the top card, naming the fraction, and placing a small object over the matching picture on a board. Cards are returned to the bottom of the pile. Play can continue until a row, column, or whole board is filled.

Get some small counters.
Play this game with a family member.

Board 1   Board 2

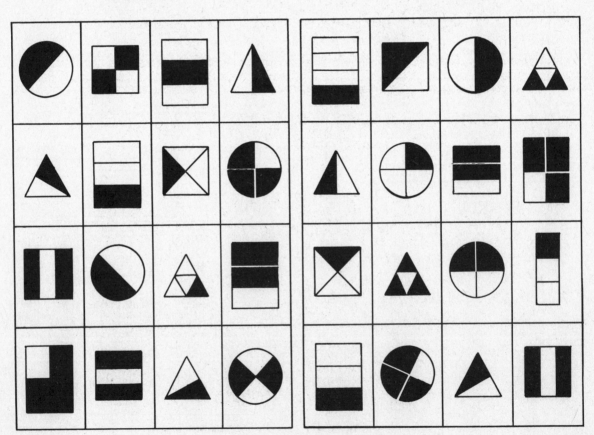

Larger Sets

1. $\frac{1}{2}$ is shaded.

Color $\frac{1}{2}$.

2. $\frac{1}{3}$ is shaded.

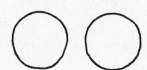

Color $\frac{1}{3}$.

3. $\frac{1}{4}$ is shaded.

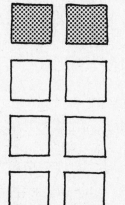

Color $\frac{1}{4}$.

Name _____

School Supplies

Read the problem. Write the data that fits
on the missing tag. Use this data:

| 10¢ | 25¢ | 30¢ | 35¢ |

Draw an **X** on the data as you use it. Add to check.

1. Lisa bought a
pencil and an
eraser. She spent
20¢ in all.

_____
_____
+ _____
_____

2. Rosa bought a
pencil and a
ruler. She spent
40¢ in all.

_____
+ _____
_____

3. Ed bought scissors
and glue. He spent
65¢ in all.

_____
_____
+ _____
_____

4. Gus bought a pen
and a pad. He
spent 50¢ in all.

_____
_____
+ _____
_____